Praise for *Re*

"The Rev. Dr. Kelly Brown Doug
Resurrection Hope, she brings her insights as a sch...,
institution builder, and public intellectual to the question that has
haunted the church and the nation since before its inception: Will
we finally imagine, build, and inhabit a world where Black lives are
valued? Amid the troubled waters of our time, Douglas gives us a
momentous gift: a vibrant religious vocabulary that not only
illuminates how white supremacy has held our moral imaginations
captive but also orients us toward an unrealized vision of a just
future." —**Robert P. Jones, CEO of PRRI, and author,** *White Too
Long: The Legacy of White Supremacy in American Christianity*

"Thank you Rev. Kelly Brown Douglas for exposing the active
intention of white supremacy to use God to diminish, demonize,
and disappear those who have been made to believe their suffering
is God's will. Yes! It is time for the Righteous vision...the Moral
Imaginary of resurrection...recomposing the decomposed!"
—**Rev. Dr. Yvette A. Flunder, Presiding Bishop, The Fellowship
of Affirming Ministries**

"Douglas takes us with her on a journey in which she gives herself
and every other Black person in America good reason to walk away
from the Christian faith, and then tells us why she perseveres in
hope. In this, her most devastating critique of white supremacy and
passionate homage to the faith of her ancestors, Douglas dares us
to believe that it's possible to create a world in which Black lives
matter." —**The Rt. Rev. Mariann Edgar Budde, Bishop, Episcopal
Diocese of Washington**

"By addressing head-on the pervasive anti-Black aspects inherent
not only in the national ideology but also in much of our
Christian theology, my long-time friend and colleague Kelly
Brown Douglas offers a powerful, deeply personal answer to the
question of what it will take for Black life to truly matter in this
country and for God's just future to become a reality for all."
—**The Most Rev. Michael B. Curry, Presiding Bishop of
The Episcopal Church, and author,** *Love Is the Way: Holding on
to Hope in Troubling Times*

"Kelly Brown Douglas is a towering theologian in this Age of Black Lives Matter who builds on and goes beyond the profound legacies of James Cone and James Baldwin, Katie Cannon and Delores Williams! *Resurrection Hope* takes us on a courageous and visionary journey full of brilliant scholarship, political struggle, and spiritual determination. And the rich dialogue with her precious son Desmond alongside the prophetic witness of her grandmother Helen Vivian Dorsey propels us toward a future of love, laughter, and liberation!" —**Cornel West, Union Theological Seminary**

"In this deeply theological and personal book, Kelly Brown Douglas leads us on her faith journey from despair to hope as she probes the deep anti-Black narrative that pervades U.S. society through monuments and silences to affirm that not only do Black lives matter but Black lives *do* matter. This book is a moving invitation for us all to undertake this journey of faith to find a deep and sustaining resurrection hope that sits with doubt and survives with a bone-deep hope." —**Emilie M. Townes, Distinguished Professor of Womanist Ethics and Society, Vanderbilt University Divinity School**

"*Resurrection Hope* is beautiful, searing, and important. It speaks to the moment and is much like Kelly Douglas's previous book, *Stand Your Ground*, but comes to us ten years later, speaking to a larger Moment. Many books fade at mid-point or so. The chapters in this one keep building on each other, and the best chapter is the last one, on cross and resurrection." —**Gary Dorrien, author, *American Democratic Socialism: History, Politics, Religion, and Theory***

"Grounded in personal engagement with our social world defined by the language and rituals of anti-Black racism, *Resurrection Hope* confronts the deep uncertainties generated by our circumstances. Douglas wrestles with religious doubt stemming from an effort to maintain the viability of faith in a context of continued Black death— and in the process forges a powerful theological understanding of our times that confronts whiteness and its depth of meaning and impact. Exposed for the reader's viewing is the warped moral imagination making possible such profound hate. Douglas calls for a reworking of our moral imaginary that opens us to practices of radical transformation. Take this theological journey with Douglas, and be all the better for it!" —**Anthony B. Pinn, author, *Interplay of Things: Religion, Art, and Presence Together***

Resurrection Hope

Resurrection Hope

A Future Where Black Lives Matter

Kelly Brown Douglas

ORBIS BOOKS
Maryknoll, New York 10545

Founded in 1970, Orbis Books endeavors to publish works that enlighten the mind, nourish the spirit, and challenge the conscience. The publishing arm of the Maryknoll Fathers and Brothers, Orbis seeks to explore the global dimensions of the Christian faith and mission, to invite dialogue with diverse cultures and religious traditions, and to serve the cause of reconciliation and peace. The books published reflect the views of their authors and do not represent the official position of the Maryknoll Society. To learn more about Maryknoll and Orbis Books, please visit our website at www.orbisbooks.com.

Manufactured in the United States of America

Library of Congress Cataloging-in-Publication Data

Names: Douglas, Kelly Brown, author.
Title: Resurrection hope : a future where Black lives matter / Kelly Brown Douglas.
Description: Maryknoll, NY : Orbis Books, [2021] | Includes bibliographical references and index. | Summary: "An exploration of the deep roots of anti-Blackness in American culture, and the gospel support for the call that "Black Lives Matter.""— Provided by publisher.
Identifiers: LCCN 2021018225 (print) | LCCN 2021018226 (ebook) | ISBN 9781626984455 (trade paperback) | ISBN 9781608339082 (epub)
Subjects: LCSH: African Americans—Social conditions. | Black lives matter movement—Religious aspects—Christianity. | Race relations—Religious aspects—Christianity—History. | Racism—United States. | Racism—Religious aspects—Christianity—History. | United States—Race relations.
Classification: LCC E185.86 .D64 2021 (print) | LCC E185.86 (ebook) | DDC 305.800973—dc23
LC record available at https://lccn.loc.gov/2021018225
LC ebook record available at https://lccn.loc.gov/2021018226

To my partner on this journey
Lamont G. Douglas

CONTENTS

PART TWO
From Crucifying Death to Resurrection Hope

ACKNOWLEDGMENTS

This book would not have been possible without those who have accompanied and supported me on this journey. I thank Serene Jones, president of Union Theological Seminary and my sister on the journey who provides the space and encouragement to "do your work." I thank my Episcopal Divinity School at Union colleagues Ian Rees and Miguel Escobar for taking up the slack and more, allowing me to give focused attention to writing. I am especially grateful to Douglas Berger and Robin Reese, whose words of support, encouragement, and sheer affirmation, along with reminders that what I was doing mattered, came always at the right time, inspiring me to keep going.

Without the gift of my relationship of over twenty-five years with Orbis editor-in-chief (and publisher) Robert Ellsberg, one that has progressed over time to becoming friends and family, this book would not have come to fruition. Thank you, Robert, for giving me the confidence to reclaim my voice and speak my truth, and then for finding power in my words.

There are never words enough to say thank you to my spouse and partner in life, Lamont, whose unending belief in me and unconditional support have sustained me on this journey.

And then there is my son, Desmond, from whom I learn every day. His generous spirit, his courage to be who he is, and his determination to speak his truth are the source of my strength and hope. This book is his. Thank you, Desmond!

INTRODUCTION

A Journey of Faith

Anselm's dictum that theology is "faith seeking understanding" perfectly describes my theological journey. Even before I knew the word "theology," I struggled to understand the meaning of my faith in relationship to my Blackness. That struggle has been reflected in my previous writings, from *The Black Christ* (1994) to *Stand Your Ground: Black Bodies and the Justice of God* (2015). At that point, my faith journey had taken me from understanding the meaning of Jesus's birth in a manger to his death on a cross. On that journey I was affirmed in my faith that Jesus was Black and, therefore, intimately identified with the Black fight for life and wholeness in this country—a fight defined by the perverse realities of white supremacy. In discovering the Blackness of Christ, I was able to affirm my love for Jesus without contradiction, because in fact Jesus was Black like me.

Nevertheless, my struggle to affirm my faith in light of my Blackness continues for me today, though perhaps in a more focused and intense way, for while I had initially wondered about the propriety of faith in what I originally believed to be a "white Jesus," I now found myself struggling with the efficacy of faith itself. James Baldwin once said that there comes a time in the life of every Black person in America when they must face the "shock" of discovering "that the flag to which you have pledged allegiance...has not pledged allegiance to you."[1] And now, as the mother of a six-foot-tall, loc-wearing, twenty-seven-year-old Black man, fearing for his life in this nation as much as I did when he was born, and realizing the gravity of this country's "sin" that is a mortal threat to all Black life, I find myself facing the shock that perhaps the "God of Jesus Christ" in whom Black people have pledged our faith has not really "pledged allegiance to us."

That "shock" was made even more real by the questions my son asked me. As Black death was becoming more and more routine in the nation—whether at the hands of police or from the COVID-19 virus—my son challenged my faith in a Black Christ.

"How do we really know that God cares when Black people are still getting killed? How long do we have to wait for the justice of God?" he asked. "I get it, that Christ is Black, but that doesn't seem to be helping us right now."

These are the questions that I seek to answer. This book reflects my journey of faith-seeking-understanding amidst the cries of "Black Lives Matter" and the questions my son was asking me. Through this book I attempt to answer these questions by first discerning why this nation is one that "lets Black people die" and then figuring out what God has to say about it. This book is essentially a journey of faith.

Paul Tillich reminds us that "the element of uncertainty in faith cannot be removed," given that the object of our faith is transcendent, that is, beyond our human grasp.[2] Essentially,

---

1. "Debate: Baldwin vs. Buckley," June 14, 1965, Film and Media Archive, Washington University in St. Louis, Library of Congress, American Archive of Public Broadcasting (GBH and the Library of Congress), Boston, MA, and Washington, DC, http://americanarchive.org/catalog/cpb-aacip-151-sn00z71m54.

2. Paul Tillich, *Dynamics of Faith* (New York: Harper and Row, 1957; New York: Penguin Classics, 2001), 18.

Tillich is reminding us that doubt is intrinsic to faith. This book has been for me a journey through the doubts intrinsic to *my* faith, as I began to wonder whether God's promise in a just future is to be believed. Not only was it hard to live in the promise yet-to-be-fulfilled, but with each—almost daily—reminder that Black life does not matter in this nation, I no longer trusted the promise itself. And so, in this book I essentially walk through the valley of death when it comes to Black life, not knowing if on the other side I will affirm my faith or give in to despair. This is a journey from the crucifying realities of Black death to an attempt to find the resurrection hope of Black life.

The book is divided into two parts. Part 1 reflects the "valley of the shadow of death" that is signaled by a "raced" moral imaginary. In this section I discover the ways in which whiteness has so corrupted the moral imaginary that it is impossible to envision a society—and perhaps even a world—where Black lives can ever truly matter. In chapter 1 I argue that if we are to understand the threat to Black life in this country we must appreciate the profound and pervasive impact of an anti-Black narrative that is inseparable from the nation's white supremacist foundation. One of the most disconcerting aspects in this part of my journey was discovering the ways in which this anti-Blackness is embedded in the very theological fabric of Christianity. What, I wonder, is to become of the moral imaginary if even Christianity itself is beholden to a theological framework that fosters death for Black bodies? In chapter 2, I turn to one of the most visible symbols of the nation's compromised moral imaginary, as well as indicators of the depth of the problem when it comes to race: the Confederate monuments on the public square. In this chapter I argue that these monuments reflect a "white way of knowing" to which the nation's moral imaginary is tethered. But what about faith leaders, the stewards of God's promise for a more just future? Chapter 3 attempts to understand the "silence" of "good white Christians" when it comes to being in utter solidarity with Black people in the quest for justice. This chapter identifies the way in which whiteness has so impacted the gaze of even "good" white Christians that it does not open them to the complex realities of Black people who "live with their backs against the wall" of white supremacy, let alone to the significance of God's revelation when it comes to the struggle for Black lives to matter. Each chapter ends by looking at the implications for the moral imaginary and the possibility of freeing it from "white knowing," and thus the possibility for a future where Black life will matter.

Part 2 is primarily theological testimony. It consists of two chapters that explore my walk from the valley of crucifying death into the hope of resurrection. Through that walk I have come to a new theological appreciation of Jesus's movement from cross to resurrection. I begin by exploring in chapter 4 what it would mean to free the moral imaginary from a white knowing. What are the implications for a faith that places a crucified and resurrected savior at its center? I explore this in relation to reparations, with special attention to the call to "defund the police." The focus is on the implications for the faith community, especially the white faith community. Chapter 5 represents the culmination of the journey. In this chapter I heed the call of the resurrected Jesus to meet him in Galilee. It is in the "Galilee" of a Black Lives Matter protest that I discover the truth of "resurrection hope" that is God's promise.

And so, as much as this book is about a nation's story, it is also about my own story. It is a personal journey in which my son's questions pressed me to struggle with the very meaning of my faith, and not to run from the doubts. Through this book, I invite you to take that journey with me.

PART ONE

A CORRUPTED MORAL IMAGINARY

"I Am Trayvon." "Say Her Name." "Hands Up Don't Shoot." "I Can't Breathe." "Black Lives Matter." These mantras filled my mind as I answered the call to run 2.23 miles to honor and demand justice for Ahmaud Arbery, who was gunned down by two white men as he was jogging in a Georgia suburb.[1]

By the time I completed the run, I was breathless—but not because my legs were tired or my lungs were winded. I was breathless because my heart was heavy and my spirit was troubled. Ahmaud had become the latest in a long list of young Black lives lost to the hatred of white racist violence. Then there was Breonna Taylor, killed in her own home in Louisville.[2] Next came the videos of George Floyd uttering those fateful words, "I can't breathe," before calling out for his "Mama," while pinned under the deadly knee of a white police officer.[3] As I was taking

---

1. On May 8, 2020, which would have been Ahmaud Arbery's 26th birthday, supporters from around the world ran 2.23 miles, representing the date of Ahmaud's murder on February 23.

2. Breonna Taylor, 26 years old, was killed on March 13, 2020, in Louisville, Kentucky, when police executed a no-knock warrant at her home shortly after midnight.

3. George Floyd, 46, was killed on May 25, 2020, in Minneapolis, Minnesota, during an arrest for allegedly passing a counterfeit bill.

in all of this horror, I was also haunted by my son's question: "Do you really believe that Black life will ever truly matter in this country?"

As I pondered the expendable nature of Black life in American society, I became increasingly aware that the threat to Black life comes not just from the white supremacist foundation upon which this country was built. What I found myself contemplating was the corrupted soul of the nation.

The soul signifies the human connection to a divine creator; it connects human beings to their higher, aspirational selves. It is that which animates and propels humans to do better and to be better. The soul is that imperceptible aspect of the human creature which indicates its vital moral core. It pushes humans toward the fullest potential of what it means to be "just," thus propelling them in reflecting the just and loving God in whose image they were created. The soul is the essence of that divinely created humanity within each human being.

The human soul is not defined by the unpredictable and vacillating protestations of society, nor is it accountable to the politics and prejudices of human history. Rather, it is responsive to a vision of justice that stands above the biased considerations of a nation at any given time. The soul is inextricably bound to the transcendent "moral arc of the universe, that bends toward justice" — a justice that is nothing other than the perfect justice of God.

It was perhaps that conception of the human soul that Abraham Lincoln invoked in his first inaugural address, stating that he hoped that the nation would be "touched" by "the better angels of our nature." In effect, he was suggesting that a nation has something analogous to the human soul — a vital moral core that propels a nation, as it does a human person, toward its highest aspirational self. In the case of a nation, that would be a future in which all human beings are treated with equal dignity and, therefore, respected as the divinely created beings that we all are.

This brings us to the question: What has corrupted the very soul of America, resulting not only in routine violence against Black lives, but also in preventing people from simply reaching for their best selves and treating others, no matter how "raced," with decency and compassion? The answer: whiteness itself.

As I have argued in previous texts, whiteness is not a biological or an ethnic given. Rather, it is a socially constructed demarcation of race that serves as a badge of privilege and power. It fuels white supremacy, which in turn exists to protect it. White supremacy is the network of systemic, structural, and ideological realities that protect the "presumed" superiority of whiteness by granting certain privileges to those raced white and not to others. These are the privileges of social, political, economic, and even personal entitlements, such as claiming space and "standing one's ground." It is in this way that whiteness signals social relationships of power. It defines the relationship between those who represent the "privileged dominant caste" (signaled by whiteness) and those who represent the "subjugated caste" (signaled by Blackness).[4]

Whiteness is an inherently oppositional construct. Its existence, indeed its power, is characteristically defined in antagonistic opposition to groups not raced white, thereby threatening the "unalienable rights" of the non-white other (*their* rights to "life, liberty, and the pursuit of happiness"). Anything that belittles, degrades, or betrays the sacred humanity of another is violent and, insofar as it separates one from the ways of a just and loving God, sinful. Whiteness, therefore, is both an intrinsically violent and sinful construct.

In the final analysis, whiteness is soul-crushing. In an obvious way it crushes the souls of those whom whiteness *others*. But

---

4. Isabel Wilkerson speaks of these power relationships as indicative of a caste system baked into America's social/political fabric, much like the caste system of India. See *Caste: The Origins of Our Discontents* (New York: Random House, 2020).

it also hinders people consumed by and enamored with the privileges of being raced white from reaching for their better selves. Those who remain willfully or obliviously trapped in the privileges of whiteness are prevented from appreciating their common connection with the rest of humanity. In effect, uninterrupted whiteness overwhelms white people's very souls, foiling their ability to live into the urgings of their "better angels."

In regard to America's soul, while it is inextricably related to and shaped by the historically dominant cultural group (that is, the group that has defined the nation's very sense of self), it is about more than the way a particular people adjudicates whiteness. Indeed, the soul of the nation is not even defined by whether or not individuals consider themselves racist or antiracist. Rather it is shaped, in this instance, by the way in which whiteness has so penetrated and defined the nation's foundation that it ultimately impacts its vision of justice and thereby affects the nation's moral impulses across succeeding generations. Simply put, the state of the nation's soul is reflected in the nation's moral imaginary (to which we shall return).

For now, what is important to note is that while the reality of whiteness—which manifests as white supremacy—has, from America's origins, shaped the nation's laws, policies, social-cultural relationships, and fundamental ethos, this nation, at the same time, was able to cultivate a higher vision for an equitable and just society. This is the aforementioned vision which contends that all persons are created equal with certain "unalienable rights." The sheer fact that this vision was ever even articulated (albeit as a part of the Declaration of Independence and not the Constitution itself) reflects a force beyond the biases of a people trapped in their own whiteness. As fleeting a vision as it may have been (even within the Declaration, as we will later see), it at least indicates the urgings of the nation's soul, pushing its founders and framers beyond their white presumptions and ideologies toward an unbiased sense of justice. It was this "soul"-driven vision that Martin Luther King Jr. referred to as the "promissory note" on which, when it came to its Black citizens, America had "defaulted." This note, he said, "was a promise that all men, yes, black men as well as white men, would be guaranteed the 'unalienable Rights' of 'Life, Liberty and the pursuit of Happiness.'"[5]

Unfortunately, this vision of an equitable and just nation was corrupted from its very inception by the pervasive reality of whiteness intrinsic to America's foundation, and thus, baked into its very Constitution. The white supremacist bent of this nation is most evident in the U.S. Constitution's Fugitive Slave Clause, Article 4, Section 2, which reads:

> No Person held to Service or Labour in one State, under the Laws thereof, escaping into another, shall, in Consequence of any Law or Regulation therein, be discharged from such Service or Labour, but shall be delivered up of Claim of the Party to whom such Service or Labour may be due.[6]

It would not be until the passage of the Fourteenth Amendment to the Constitution that this clause would be nominally annulled. With the Fourteenth and other Reconstruction-era Amendments the nation at last began to gesture toward the reality of an American identity beyond the "Caucasian race," a nation not simply meant "for white men."[7]

It cannot be stressed enough that whiteness is integral to America's sense of self. A belief in the superiority of whiteness was essentially a given in the minds of the founders and framers, thus assuring the inevitability of white supremacist

---

5. *American Rhetoric: Top 100 Speeches,* "Martin Luther King, Jr., 'I Have a Dream,'" https://www.americanrhetoric.com/speeches/mlkihaveadream.htm.

6. https://constitutioncenter.org/interactive-constitution/article/article-iv.

7. Eric Foner, *The Second Founding: How the Civil War and Reconstruction Remade the Constitution* (New York: W. W. Norton and Company Inc., 2019), chapter 2, esp. pp. 86ff.

structures and systems. It is no overstatement to say that white supremacy is the normative identifying marker of American identity. The insidious consequence of this is that the belief in white superiority is embedded within the collective consciousness of America and has been from its earliest beginnings. Because of this, whiteness has not only produced what theologian Willie Jennings calls "a social imaginary," but it has also profoundly affected the nation's "moral imaginary."

The "imaginary" is different from the imagination. It is suggestive of more than an idea or conception. The imaginary reflects the zeitgeist, that is, the characteristic propensity and inclination of a nation. The moral imaginary reflects the nation's moral impulse. It is the reflexive moral response, that is, the nation's organic reaction to social issues and concerns. Essentially, the moral imaginary is that palpable yet imperceptible force that defines the way in which a nation intuitively perceives and responds to matters of injustice as well as the way it envisions and enacts justice. As suggested earlier, the moral imaginary is conspicuously shaped by the group that has been historically, culturally, and socially dominant in a nation. In the words of Erich Fromm, "In any society the spirit [i.e., imaginary] of the whole culture is determined by the spirit of those groups that are most powerful in that society."[8] As for America, borrowing from the words of Reinhold Niebuhr, "the natural impulse by which [American] society achieves its [moral] cohesion," is whiteness.[9]

As whiteness has compromised the soul of America, it has inexorably impacted its moral imaginary. Whiteness has prevented the nation from living from its soul into the vision of a land of equal justice for all; at times, it has even inhibited its ability to gesture toward such a vision. A non-raced vision of justice

8. Erich Fromm, *Escape from Freedom* (New York/Toronto: Rinehart and Company, Inc., 1941), 112–13.

9. Niebuhr, *Moral Man and Immoral Society* (New York: Charles Scribners's Sons, 1932), xii.

exceeds the possibilities of a white moral imaginary. Whiteness has so stifled the nation's moral imaginary that a true non-racialized democratic society of equality pushes it beyond its limits. America's old "wineskins" of whiteness cannot contain a society where there is justice and freedom for all. Whiteness has so impacted the nation's soul that white privileging and justice have become reflexively synonymous within the nation's moral imaginary.

In 2016 nearly half of American voters (victorious because of the Electoral College) embraced a vision of American "greatness" rooted in whiteness. That an even larger number of Americans doubled down on this choice four years later signaled the troubling state of America's soul—and thus its profoundly "raced" moral imaginary. In Part 1 of this book we will look at the varied impacts and implications of a "raced" moral imaginary.

1

Anti-Blackness: More Than White Privilege

"Just saw the video of police killing yet another Black man. As always be careful, stay safe, and remember what to do if you are stopped for whatever reason by the police: hands on the steering wheel, do nothing and say nothing, stay alive."

That was the text that I sent my then twenty-three-year-old son after watching the video of Philando Castile being killed by a white police officer for no readily apparent reason during a 2016 traffic stop in Minnesota.

In response, my son texted: "Oh yeah, it didn't help Philando. So now what are we supposed to do?"

After receiving that text I immediately called my son so that I could hear the feelings behind his question. What I heard was neither fear nor despair. Instead, I heard a sobering awareness of what it means to be Black in America. It was the awareness articulated by National Basketball Association coach Doc Rivers in response to persistent police violence inflicted upon Black bodies. "It's amazing to me," he said, "why we [Black people] keep loving this country and this country does not love us back."[1]

---

1. Doc Rivers, responding to NBA protest in response to the August 23, 2020, shooting of Jacob Blake by police officers in Kenosha, Wisconsin, https://www.youtube.com/watch?v=-UjGhM_w97Q.

My son was facing the shocking awareness of the profound anti-Black narrative in this country. This narrative is distinct from, yet part and parcel of America's white supremacist foundation.

As previously noted, the routine violence of white supremacy is manifest in the systemic, structural, and cultural ways it privileges whiteness and penalizes those who are not raced white. However, such privileges and penalties do not adequately account for the visceral assaults, sometimes fatal, upon Black bodies. These consistent, malicious attacks, while grounded in whiteness, reflect more than a belief in the superiority of whiteness. Such attacks bespeak a singular, deep-seated fear of, if not contempt for, Blackness itself.

Whiteness as a construct exists only in opposition to that which is non-white. In this regard, it finds its most oppositional counterpart in Blackness. The construct of whiteness thus provides fertile soil for what is perhaps the inevitable flourishing of an anti-Black narrative. Whether inevitable or not, it is only in appreciating the pervasive and distinctive presence and dehumanizing presuppositions of an anti-Black narrative ensconced within this country's collective psyche that we can begin to understand the intensity of white repulsion when it comes to Black bodies.

This chapter explores the roots of America's anti-Black narrative within ancient Western thought and the Christian theological infrastructure before looking at the way it has impacted the country's moral imaginary. My intent is not to provide a historical account of the development of the anti-Black narrative. Rather, it is simply to provide a general overview of the philosophical and theological underpinnings of the anti-Black narrative as a way to fathom its deep-rooted, sinister reality, and its ultimate impact on the nation's moral imaginary during the time of Black lynching at the hands of police.

The Deep Roots of an Anti-Black Narrative

The Philosophical Foundation

While the concept of "race" as we know it today does not seem to have played a part in the life of the ancient Greco-Roman world, the philosophical and cultural antecedents for an anti-Black narrative are certainly found in ancient Greco-Roman thought. This is particularly evident in the work of Aristotle, who laid the foundation for racially defined hierarchies that eventually rendered Black people inferior beings. Aristotle fostered the notion that blackness signaled an immoral if not a dangerous nature.

In an effort to justify Greek ruling superiority, Aristotle argued that the climates in which people lived determined the physical, intellectual, and moral characteristics of that people. He explained that extreme climates produced aesthetically, intellectually, and morally inferior beings. Extreme cold produced an inferior pale people (such as the Scythians), and extreme heat produced an inferior dark people (such as the Ethiopians). Moderate climates, such as that of the Greeks, produced the best people—those meant to rule. In his work *De Generatione Animalium*, after describing the "straight" hair and "fluid constitution" of the Scythians who live in moist climates, Aristotle says: "Ethiopians and people who live in hot regions have curly hair, because both their brains and the environing air are dry."[2] Noteworthy is the fact that Aristotle reserves comments about the brain for the Ethiopians. In *Physiognomics* Aristotle argues that the physical features of "black" peoples, from their complexions to their hair, are a sign of cowardice. He says, "Those who are

---

2. *Aristotle*, De Generatione Animalium, 782b, in *Generation of Animals with an English Translation*, translated by A. L. Peck (Cambridge, MA: Harvard University Press, 1943), 518, https://archive.org/details/generationofanim00arisuoft/page/n3/mode/2up?q=ethiopians.

too swarthy are cowardly; this applies to Egyptians and Ethiopians." Likewise, he argues, "Those with very woolly hair are cowardly; this applies to the Ethiopians."[3] Even though he mentions that those who are "excessively fair" are also cowardly, "witnessed" he says, by their women, he seems to place special emphasis on the fact that "an excessively black colour signifies cowardice," and this applies to both Black men and Black women.[4] Of course, in keeping with his chauvinistic views, it was those who lived in moderate climates, with a complexion between that of Scythians and that of Ethiopians—again, his fellow Greeks—who stood apart for their courage.

Also noteworthy is the fact that in ancient and early Greco-Roman literature Ethiopia and Scythia were viewed as being geographically polar opposites. For instance, in his *Odyssey* Homer describes the Ethiopians as a people "who are at the world's end."[5] Drawing upon the work of earlier Greek historians and writers, the ancient Greek geographer Strabo described the locations of Ethiopia and Scythia this way: "The nation of the Ethiopians stretches from the winter sunrise to sunset, and . . . Scythia lies directly opposite in the north."[6] Perhaps already developing, therefore, was an antagonistically defined ideological framework for contrasting the "fairest"-skinned and darkest-skinned people —a precursor to the racial oppositionality between whiteness and Blackness. The geographical polarity between Scythia and Ethiopia

---

3. Aristotle, *Physiognomics*, 812a, 812b, in *Aristotle: Minor Works*, translated by W. S. (Walter Stanley) Hett (Cambridge, MA: Harvard University Press, 1936), https://babel.hathitrust.org/cgi/pt?id=mdp.39015008364088&view=1up&seq=142&q1=excessively%20black%20colour.

4. Aristotle, *Physiognomics*, 812a.

5. Homer, *Odyssey, Book 1*, translated by Samuel Butler, https://www.gutenberg.org/files/1727/1727-h/1727-h.htm#chap01.

6. The *Geography of Strabo, Greek Texts with Facing English Translation* by H. L. Jones, 8 vols., Loeb Classical Library (Cambridge, MA: Harvard University Press, 1917–1932), 1:1.2.28, https://penelope.uchicago.edu/Thayer/E/Roman/Texts/Strabo/1B2*.html.

notwithstanding, Ethiopia was considered the region farthest removed from Greek culture, and hence Ethiopians were considered the most remote people—not only geographically but also culturally, intellectually, and morally.

The view of Ethiopia as geographically remote suggested an intrinsic character flaw in its inhabitants, a flaw resulting in the grave moral depravity of its Black-skinned people—especially in comparison to the Greeks and even the Scythians. This was in keeping with the fact that Blackness itself had long before come to symbolize evil or bad character. For instance, the Greek poet Pindar described one who has turned away from God as having a "black heart, with its frozen flame."[7] In his *Moralia*, Plutarch, quoting Pythagoras, advised the young: "Do not spend your time with men of black character, because of their malevolence."[8]

Furthermore, in early Greek thought blackness marked Ethiopians not only as disreputable but also as hypersexual. In the early Greco-Roman world, Ethiopian males were caricatured as macro-phallic and the females as sexual temptresses. This is significant given the fact that a hypersexual trope is a salient feature of the anti-Black narrative that besets Black Americans. The seeds of this trope were thus sown in the Greco-Roman world. Early Christian literature would also foster this trope.

Before looking at Christian literature, however, it is important to note how another ancient, dark-skinned people, the Egyptians, were viewed. Even though the Egyptians were not considered to be as geographically remote as the Ethiopians and were often highly regarded in ancient mythological and Greek literature, they would not escape the evil and questionable character associated with Blackness. Strabo, for instance,

---

7. *The Odes of Pindar, Including the Principal Fragments*, translated with an introduction by John Edwin Sandys (London: W. Heinemann/New York: The Macmillan Co., 1915), 641, https:// babel.hathitrust.org/cgi/pt?id=uc1. 32106009292506&view=1up&seq=640& q1=black.

8. Plutarch, *Moralia*, Volume 1, translated by Frank Cole Babbit, Loeb Library Classic (Cambridge, MA: Harvard University Press, 1986), 59.

described them as "quick-tempered."[9] Josephus, in *Against Apion*, best captures the perception of the Egyptians in the Greco-Roman world. In refuting Apion's claims that his adversaries were Jewish and that he himself was not, Josephus writes:

> That he should lie about our ancestors and assert that they were Egyptians by race is by no means surprising. He told a lie which was the reverse of this one about himself. Born in the Egyptian oasis, more Egyptian than them all, as one might say, he disowned his true country and falsely claimed to be an Alexandrian, thereby admitting the ignominy of his race. It is therefore natural that he should call persons whom he detests and wishes to abuse Egyptians. Had he not had the meanest opinion of natives of Egypt, he would never have turned his back on his own nation. (Book 2.3)

In brief, by the end of the Roman period, Egyptians as well as Ethiopians were often considered an ignominious people and described in increasingly pejorative terms. These understandings were based upon their "blackness." Stereotypes like these, as biblical scholar Gay Byron argues, would find their way into the "ideological infrastructure of ancient [and early] Christian writings,"[10] thus providing sacred legitimation for anti-Blackness. To this we will now turn.

The Christian Foundation

While anti-Black overtones were present in the writings of various early church fathers, Origen's views, according to those who study this period, "would become standard Christian ideas

---

9. Strabo, *Geography*, 8:17.1.12.

10. Gay L. Byron, *Symbolic Blackness and Ethnic Difference in Early Christian Literature* (London/New York: Routledge, 2002), 125.

about Ethiopians."[11] Like Aristotle, Origen connects a people's character to climate. He states that extreme climates are associated with an inferior people, while moderate climates (not too hot or too cold) are associated with a more superior people. Going beyond Aristotle, however, Origen argues that the fact that certain people live in extreme environments in the first place indicates their sinful nature. Essentially, the environment in which people are located is a result of their intrinsic worthiness or lack thereof. It was in this way that for Origen Blackness came to be a sign of a sinful soul. Origen's "Commentary" on the Song of Songs makes clear the connection between Blackness and sin.

In trying to make sense of the bride's exclamation, "I am dark and beautiful," Origen states: "It can be said also of each individual soul that turns to repentance after many sins, that she is black by reason of the sins, but beautiful through her repentance and the fruits of her repentance."[12] This point is made even more explicit in a homily on the same topic. He says, "We understand, then, why the Bride is black and beautiful at one and the same time. But, if you do not likewise practise penitence, take heed lest *your* soul be described as black and ugly, and you be hideous with a double foulness—black by reason of your past sins and ugly because you are continuing in the same vices!"[13] Simply put, for Origen Blackness signals a sinful soul that can be saved, that is made white through conversion to Christianity; hence, an Ethiopian can be saved. In the words of Hellenistic scholar Aaron P. Johnson, for Origen, "Ethiopian identity, allegorically understood, is the pre-conversion state of a soul; it is

11. Aaron P. Johnson, "The Blackness of Ethiopians: Classical Ethnography and Eusebius's Commentary on the Psalms," *The Harvard Theological Review* 99, no. 2 (2006): 165–86 at 170, JSTOR, www.jstor.org/stable/4125292.

12. "The Commentary," in *The Song of Songs, Commentary and Homilies*, translated and annotated by R. P. Lawson (New York/Mahwah, NJ: The Newman Press, 1956), 106.

13. "The Commentary," 276.

an identity to be shunned, a sinful darkness to be washed in the whitening process of conversion."[14] We should note, however, that in Origen's later writings Ethiopians are associated with "demonic forces" beyond redemption.

As earlier suggested, these anti-Black overtones are present in the writings of other church fathers. For instance, Tertullian also associates both the Egyptians and Ethiopians with sin. He argues, "When God...threatens destruction to Egypt and Ethiopia, He surely pre-condemns every sinning nation, whatever. If, reasoning from species to genus, every nation that sins against them is an Egypt and Ethiopia."[15]

In his Homily on Psalm 86, Jerome is even more explicit on the connection between Ethiopian Blackness and sin. He describes Ethiopia "as black and cloaked in the filth of sin." He goes on to say, "At one time we were all Ethiopians in our vices and sins. How so? Because our sins had blackened us. But afterwards we heard the words: 'Wash yourselves clean!' And we said: 'Wash me, and I shall be whiter than snow.' We are Ethiopians, therefore, who have been transformed from blackness into whiteness."[16]

The view of Blackness as a signifier for sin is even more pronounced in the portrayal of demonic beings as Black. Early Christian literature is replete with images of the devil as Black. For instance, the Epistle of Barnabas cast the devil as the "Black One." It says, "Wherefore let us take heed in these last days. For the whole time of our faith shall profit us nothing, unless we now, in the season of lawlessness and in the offenses that shall be, as becometh sons of God, offer resistance, that the Black

---

14. "Blackness of Ethiopians," 173.

15. Tertullian, *De spectaculis*, chapter 3, http://www.tertullian.org/anf/anf03/anf03-09.htm.

16. Saint Jerome, *The Homilies of Saint Jerome*, translated by Marie Liguori Ewald (Washington: Catholic University of America Press, 1964), 140.

One may not effect an entrance."[17] The Epistle goes on to say that "the way of the Black One is crooked and full of a curse. For it is a way of eternal death with punishment wherein are the things that destroy men's souls—idolatry, boldness, exhalation of power, hypocrisy, doubleness of heart, adultery, murder, plundering, pride, transgression, treachery, malice, stubbornness, witchcraft, magic, covetousness, absence of the fear of God."[18]

The Acts of Peter goes even further as it casts the tempting devil not simply as Black, but as an Ethiopian woman: "For just now when I turned myself to sleep for a little, I beheld thee sitting in a high place and before thee a great multitude, and a woman exceeding foul, in sight like an Ethiopian, not an Egyptian, but altogether black and filthy, clothed in rags, and with an iron collar about her neck and chains upon her hands and feet, dancing."[19]

These early epistles and Christian narratives notwithstanding, there are probably no writings in which Blackness is more associated with the demonic than those of the Desert Fathers. In these writings the tropes of anti-Blackness are fully present. Not only are Ethiopians demonized because of their color but they are also depicted as hypersexual, and hence, sexually immoral and dangerous threats to the virtue of others.

Interestingly, however, there was an Ethiopian among the Desert Fathers, Abba Moses. He, like the Bride of Solomon, was able to overcome his mark of Blackness—though he would be consistently put to the test because of it.

---

17. "The Epistle of Barnabas," 4.9, translated by J. B. Lightfoot, http://www.earlychristianwritings.com/text/barnabas-lightfoot.html.

18. "The Epistle of Barnabas," 20.1.

19. "The Acts of Peter," from *The Apocryphal New Testament*, translated with notes by M. R. James (Oxford: Clarendon Press, 1924), xxii, http://www.earlychristianwritings.com/text/actspeter.html.

After leading a sinful life as a murderer and robber, Moses repented and joined one of the desert monasteries. While he has come to be valued in Christian hagiography for his obedience and virtue, during his lifetime he was tested on numerous occasions in order to prove that he had overcome his "Blackness." It is reported that on one occasion, when joining a council of fellow abbots, "the Fathers treated Moses with contempt in order to test him, saying, 'Why does this black man come among us?'"[20]

It is written that on another occasion, that of his ordination as a priest, after the ephod was placed upon him, "The archbishop said to him, 'See, Abba Moses, now you are entirely white.' The old man [Moses] said to him, 'It is true of the outside, lord and father, but what about Him who sees the inside?' Wishing to test him, the archbishop said to the priests, 'When Abba Moses comes into the sanctuary, drive him out, and go with him to hear what he says.' So the old man came in and they covered him with abuse and drove him out, saying, 'Outside, black man!' Going out, he said to himself, 'They have acted rightly concerning you. For your skin is as black as ashes. You are not a man, so why would you be allowed to meet men?'"[21] In the end, Abba Moses's Blackness was depicted as a persistent point of contention not only for his fellow priests but for himself as well. It is interesting to note that even today he is often referred to as St. Moses the Black, suggesting still the paradox of being "holy" yet Black.

The stories of St. Anthony of Egypt, considered the father of monastic monks, provide even clearer examples of the Black Ethiopian demonic figure in monastic literature. In *The Life of St. Anthony* by St. Athanasius, classicist scholar David Brakke identifies "the devil's appearance as a black boy," as the "earliest datable appearance of a black (or Ethiopian) demon in monastic

---

20. Benedicta Ward, *The Sayings of the Desert Fathers: The Alphabetical Collection*, rev. ed. (Kalamazoo, MI: Cistercian Publications, 1984), 139.

21. Ward, *The Sayings of the Desert Fathers*, 139.

literature," again replete with hypersexual tropes.[22] In this work, Athanasius reports that in a last-ditch effort to get a young Anthony to succumb to sinful temptation, the devil, having previously taken the form of a woman, appears as a "black boy, taking a visible shape in accordance with the colour of his mind."[23] Brakke points out that, for Athanasius "the mind or rational faculty was the location of the self's true nature."[24] Implied is the devil's assumption that Anthony's mind was Black, that is, of a sinful nature. The story goes on to say that when Anthony asked the Black boy who he was, he answered, "I am the friend of whoredom. I am called the spirit of lust." Anthony responded "You are very despicable then, for you are black hearted and weak as a child." "Having heard this," Athanasius writes, "the black one straightway fled."[25]

This story is representative of the sexual trope associated with Blackness in early monastic literature, on a foundation laid by earlier representations of Ethiopians. As Brakke notes, while in Athanasius's writings about Anthony the Black boy "was not (yet) Ethiopian.... When the visual form of the black demon gained more precise definition as Ethiopian, it acquired the stereotypical traits associated with the Ethiopian body type that circulated through Greco-Roman culture, especially hypersexuality."[26]

The writings of Origen, Tertullian, and Jerome, along with the monastic stories, are just a few examples of the way in which anti-Black conceptions were present within early Christian writings.

---

22. David Brakke, "Ethiopian Demons: Male Sexuality, the Black-Skinned Other, and the Monastic Self," *Journal of the History of Sexuality* 10, no. 3/4 (2001): 501–35 at 509, JSTOR, www.jstor.org/stable/3704758.

23. *The Life of Anthony of Egypt by St. Athanasius of Alexandria*, translated by Philip Schaff and Henry Wace (1892; Scotts Valley, CA: CreateSpace Independent Publishing Platform, 2016), 8.

24. Brakke, "Ethiopian Demons," 509.

25. *Life of Anthony*, 8.

26. Brakke, "Ethiopian Demons," 511.

These anti-Black ideas carried over into the early church's heresy debates, in which heretical beliefs and sects were consistently represented as Black.[27] Hence, even within doctrinal debates fundamental to Christian theology, Blackness was associated with evil—and, more significantly, with all that was anti-Christian. The theological foundation was thus sufficiently laid for later negating the religious and spiritual identities of African peoples by viewing them as heathens in need of salvation by the most effective means available: enslavement. This would of course come to fruition with the European encroachment on the African continent.

The point of the matter is that a proto-anti-Black narrative is embedded in Christianity's theological architecture. In fact, antecedents for such a narrative can be traced to the light/dark color symbolism that is pervasive and taken for granted in the very earliest Christian literature. Brakke is right when he suggests that it was "a short step" from "the earliest surviving pieces of Christian literature" like 1 Thessalonians, where there are light/dark associations with good and evil, respectively, to "identifying the devil and evil persons as not merely darkness but black."[28] French sociologist Roger Bastide best summarizes the way in which an anti-Black narrative, complete with white/Black oppositionality, are virtually intrinsic to Christianity's theological framework when he notes:

> The greatest Christian two-part division is that of white and black. White is used to express the pure, while black expresses the diabolical. The conflict between Christ and Satan, the spiritual and the carnal, good and evil came finally to be expressed by the conflict between white and black, which underlines and synthesizes all the others.... Whiteness brings to mind the light, ascension into the bright realm, the immaculateness of virgin snow, the white dove of the Holy Spirit, and the trans-

---

27. See discussion in Byron, *Symbolic Blackness*, 46–47.

28. Brakke, "Ethiopian Demons," 507.

parency of limpid air; blackness suggests the infernal streams of the bowels of the earth, the pit of hell, the devil's color.[29]

With such pervasive anti-Black theological symbolism, a whitening of Christian symbols was inevitable, including white-washing Jesus. Bastide speaks to this:

> Although Christ transcends all questions of race or ethnology, it must not be forgotten that God incarnated himself in a man of the Jewish race.... The entire history of Western painting bears witness to the deliberate whitening or bleaching effort that changed Christ from a Semitic to an Aryan person. The dark hair that Christ was thought to have had came to be rendered as very light-colored, and his big dark eyes as blue. It was necessary that this man, the incarnation of God, be as far removed as possible from everything that could suggest darkness or blackness, even indirectly. His hair and his beard were given the color of sunshine, the brightness of the light above, while his eyes retained the color of the sky from which he descended and to which he returned.
>
> The progressive Aryanization of Christ is in strict accordance with the logic of the color symbolism.[30]

Given the anti-Black symbolism ingrained within Christianity, it was perhaps an even shorter step to the eighteenth-century religious racism that emerged in order to legitimate making chattel slaves of African peoples. For instance, conjectures that Black people were not of the created line of Adam and Eve, or that their enslavement was a just punishment tracing back to the indiscretion of Ham looking upon the naked body of his father Noah (even as enslavement was considered

---

29. Roger Bastide, "Color, Racism, and Christianity," *Daedalus* 96, no. 2 (1967), 312–27 at 314–15, JSTOR, www.jstor.org/stable/20027040.

30. Bastide, "Color, Racism, and Christianity," 315.

the vehicle to salvation), were consonant with the long-held notion that Blackness itself was a sign of innate depravity.

The legacy of anti-Blackness within the Christian theological framework remains evident today in various hymns that are part of the Christian tradition. These are hymns such as "Fairest Lord Jesus," that proclaims: "Jesus is fairer, Jesus is purer" and that "Jesus shines brighter and Jesus shines purer." And then there are versions of the evangelical hymn, "Washed as White as Snow" which proclaims: "Praise the Lord, I am washed / In the all-cleansing blood of the Lamb / And my robes are whiter than the driven snow / I am washed in the blood of the Lamb." Or the hymn "Washed in the Blood of the Lamb" that asks: "Are you washed in the blood / in the soul cleansing blood of the Lamb? / Are your garments spotless? / Are they white as snow? / Are you washed in the blood of the Lamb?"

The fact that these hymns continue to exist as a part of Christian hymnody today reveals the way in which anti-Black concepts have become virtually normative within Christianity's theological culture—so much so that they go unnoticed and hence unquestioned. Moreover, scripture passages that maintain the light/dark dichotomy continue to be read, without interrogation or even acknowledgement of their anti-Black implications. I am not suggesting that these scriptural texts should not be read. However, I am suggesting that the implications of this dichotomy when it comes to fostering anti-Black sentiments should at least be acknowledged and interrogated.

As we will soon see, this almost oblivious acceptance of anti-Black precursors has been consequential in shaping the moral imaginary and subsequent attitudes and assaults on Black bodies. For now, it is important to recognize that anti-Black beliefs, if not theories, can be found in ancient Greco-Roman literature as well as within Christianity's theological structure. Let us now look briefly at the way in which anti-Black thought has penetrated Western culture.

The Anti-Black Narrative and the Black Body

We see the echoes of an anti-Black narrative in Gomes Eanes de Zurara's oft-cited description of the first captive Africans to arrive on Portuguese soil in 1444. He says: "And these, placed all together in that field, were a marvellous sight; for amongst them were some white enough, fair to look upon, and well proportioned; others were less white like mulattoes; others again were as black as Ethiops, and so ugly, both in features and in body, as almost to appear (to those who saw them) the images of a lower hemisphere."[31]

In this description Zurara equates black skin with a demonic ugliness. That he does so in an almost taken-for-granted manner suggests that such a linkage was already prevalent within the cultural ethos of fifteenth-century Europe. His description continues the trope of Ethiopians as demonic, furthering the notion that to be as Black as the Ethiopians was to be virtually beyond redemption. Most importantly, Zurara's description once again makes clear that white repugnance toward the Black body reflects more than a chauvinistic aesthetic preference. Comments regarding aesthetic "Blackness" are historically fraught with assumptions about character and temperament. Hence, it cannot be emphasized enough that white repugnance toward the Black body has rarely if ever been benign. This fact becomes even clearer in the English encounter with Africa.

By the time the English pillaged Africa for its human and natural resources, an anti-Black narrative was fully entrenched. For in many respects, as the Europeans brought their Euro-white gaze to the African continent, they also brought with them the concept of race. Instead of seeing Africa as a continent of many

---

31. Edgar Prestage, *The Chronicles of Fernão Lopes and Gomes Eanes de Zurara* (Watford, UK: Voss and Michael Ltd., 1928) 86.

nations, cultures, tribes, and diverse peoples, they saw it as a land with creatures radically different from themselves. In the white gaze of the Europeans, the Africans were not Yoruba, Eboe, or any other particular people; rather they were all "Black."

When coupled with the dissimilarity of dress and customs, not to speak of religions, the Blackness of the Africans convinced the European pillagers of a difference that was more than skin-deep. Blackness signaled to them a people who were so thoroughly uncouth that they were more beastly than human, and most certainly not created in the image of God. These sentiments are evident in travelogues from that period, such as that of sixteenth-century English geographer and promoter of English imperialism Richard Hakluyt.

After clarifying that the people of the "middle parts of Africa" were those who were once referred to as Ethiopians, he describes the Africans as "a people of *beastly* [emphasis mine] living, without a God, lawe, religion, or common wealth, and so scorched and vexed with the heat of the sunne, that in many places they curse it when it riseth."[32]

In Hakluyt's description we see again the use of the Ethiopian trope to signify utter depravity as captured by the label "beastly." This descriptor in fact implied not only that they were wild and uncivilized but also that they were hypersexualized. As Winthrop Jordan points out, the terms "beastial" and "beastly" carried with them sexual connotations. Thus, when an Englishman described the Africans as beastly, "he was frequently as much registering a sense of sexual shock as describing swinish manners."[33] Serving to reinforce this anti-Black thinking was the

---

32. Richard Hakluyt and Edmund Goldsmid, *The Principal Navigations, Voyages, Traffiques and Discoveries of the English Nation*, Vol. 11, 94, https://online books.library.upenn.edu/webbin/metabook? id=hakluyt.

33. Winthrop D. Jordan, *White over Black: American Attitudes toward the Negro, 1550–1812*, published for the Omohundro Institute of Early American

unfortunate circumstance that the Europeans' first encounter with the people of Africa coincided with their first encounters with the African apes. It required, therefore, only a small leap in the European mind to conceive of an inherent connection between the African "apes" and the African people. Once such a tie was forged, it was an even smaller leap of logic for the Europeans to assume, as Jordan remarks, "a beastly copulation or conjuncture" between the two species.[34]

The seeds planted in ancient literature had now fully sprouted. The European view of the Africans was the inevitable legacy of the ancient narratives regarding the Ethiopians. Moreover, with the explicit branding of the Africans as beasts, a foundation was laid for viewing Black people as those who need to be patrolled and controlled so as to safeguard civilized humanity — that is, white people.

That these anti-Black notions were in fact widespread among the general European public is evident in highly regarded works, such as those of William Shakespeare. The way in which Shakespeare depicts his "black" characters signals a prevailing cultural understanding of "Blackness" in Renaissance Europe, even as he ensures the ongoing deployment of anti-Black notions. We see this in the two most developed Black characters in Shakespeare's corpus: Aaron in *Titus Andronicus* and Othello, in the play of the same name.

Aaron is the embodiment of evil throughout *Titus Andronicus*. He is responsible for the trouble and wretchedness that besieges the entire Andronicus family. He frames Titus's sons for murder, and he helps to mastermind the rape of Titus's daughter, Lavinia. Admitting his evil misdeeds, Aaron regrets only that there wasn't sufficient time to commit more. He says, "But

---

History and Culture, Williamsburg, Virginia (Chapel Hill: University of North Carolina Press, 2013), 32.

34. Jordan, *White over Black*, 31.

I have done a thousand dreadful things. / As willingly as one would kill a fly, / And nothing grieves me heartily indeed, / But that I cannot do ten thousand more."[35]

Aaron remains unrepentant of his villainy to the end, repenting only of any good deed he may have perchance performed: "Ah, why should wrath be mute and fury dumb? / I am no baby, I, that with base prayers / I should repent the evils I have done. / Ten thousand worse than ever yet I did / Would I perform, if I might have my will. / If one good deed in all my life I did, / I do repent it from my very soul."[36]

Throughout the play, Aaron's villainous behavior is associated with his being a Black-skinned Moor. In describing Aaron's son, born of an illicit affair, the nurse likens him to "a devil," "a joyless, dismal, black, and sorrowful issue."[37] Later, when pleading for his son's life, Aaron connects Blackness with ignominy before going on to detail his evil acts: "And if it please thee? Why, assure thee, Lucius, / 'Twill vex thy soul to hear what I shall speak; / For I must talk of murders, rapes, and massacres, / Acts of black night, abominable deeds, / Complots of mischief, treason, villainies, / Ruthful to hear, yet piteously perform'd."[38]

The point here is that, in *Titus Andronicus*, Shakespeare is at ease with and does not challenge the stereotypes associated with Blackness. By not challenging them, he actually furthers their salience.

The same can be said of *Othello*. Admittedly, there is much debate concerning whether or not the character Othello chal-

---

35. William Shakespeare, *Titus Andronicus*, edited by Barbara A. Mowat and Paul Werstine, 5.1.143–146, https://shakespeare.folger.edu/downloads/pdf/othello_PDF_FolgerShakespeare.pdf.

36. Shakespeare, *Titus Andronicus*, 5.3.184–190.

37. Shakespeare, *Titus Andronicus*, 4.2.66, 69.

38. Shakespeare, *Titus Andronicus*, 5.1.62–66.

lenges or affirms the depravity associated with Blackness.[39] Nevertheless, it is Othello's Blackness that Iago points to as disqualifying in Othello's marriage to Brabantio's daughter, Desdemona. When alerting Brabantio to the couple's elopement, Iago uses lewd imagery invoking the trope of lustful Blackness. He says to Brabantio, "Even now, now, very now, an old black ram / Is tupping your white ewe. Arise, arise!"[40] He goes on to describe Othello as a "devil."[41] Roderigo, a would-be suitor of Desdemona, supports Iago in warning Brabantio that his daughter is in the "gross clasps of a lascivious Moor."[42]

While it is Iago, not Othello, who is the villain in the drama, it is Othello's passions that bring the play to its tragic end. His love for Desdemona coupled with the jealously that Iago provokes in him lead Othello to kill Desdemona and then himself. In the end, therefore, Othello does not overcome the trope of Black people being governed more by lustful and dangerous passion than by reason. This is especially pronounced inasmuch as Othello's falling prey to Iago's lies regarding Desdemona's infidelity defies credulity, given Othello's love for her. Othello admits to being overruled by irrational passion when in his final speech he says, of himself, "Of one that loved not wisely, but too well; / Of one not easily jealous, but being wrought."[43]

What makes Shakespeare's depiction of Blackness most dangerous over time, however, is not simply that he reinforced anti-Black tropes. Rather, it is that his work is studied as an essential

---

39. See, for instance, the discussion in Emily C. Bartels, "Making More of the Moor: Aaron, Othello, and Renaissance Refashionings of Race," *Shakespeare Quarterly* 41, no. 4 (1990): 433–54, JSTOR, www.jstor.org/stable/2870775.

40. William Shakespeare, *Othello*, edited by Barbara Mowat and Paul Werstine, 1.1.97–98, https://shakespeare.folger.edu/downloads/pdf/othello_PDF_FolgerShakespeare.pdf.

41. Shakespeare, *Othello*, 1.1.100.

42. Shakespeare, *Othello*, 1.1.141.

43. Shakespeare, *Othello*, 5.2.444–445.

part of many literature courses without investigating the way in which he represents Black characters. This was the case in both my high school and college courses in which Shakespeare was studied. Again, I am not suggesting that Shakespeare be removed from school curricula. Rather, I am advocating that when studying Shakespeare's works or any other literature with anti-Black concepts there must be a critical examination of the way in which Blackness is depicted if there is ever to be a chance of interrupting the transmission of anti-Black ideology. Unquestionably, without such examination there will be a subtle reinforcement of an anti-Black narrative, allowing this narrative to penetrate and become an unwitting part of students' psyches.

The same applies in studying the work of Enlightenment thinkers. In his classic work, *An Essay Concerning Human Understanding*, John Locke conjectured that "'if Historie lie not...' then West African women had conceived babies with apes."[44] Georg Wilhelm Friedrich Hegel, in his *Philosophy of History*, argues that there is a "peculiarly African character[istic that is] difficult to comprehend." This characteristic, he says, renders the "Negro" incapable of the "realization of any objective existence," thus relegating the Negro to being simply an example of "the natural man in his completely wild and untamed state."[45] Consistent with his description of the Negro as nothing less than feral, Hegel goes on to say that "cannibalism is looked upon as quite customary and proper" for the African Negro.[46]

Immanuel Kant developed his "racial theory" in several lectures on anthropology and geography. Notwithstanding the comprehensive, if not complex, nature of his theory, his views toward the "Negro" race were fairly consistent. Indeed, Kant is

---

44. Quoted in Ibram X. Kendi, *Stamped from the Beginning: The Definitive History of Racist Ideas in America* (New York: Alfred A. Knopf, 2013), 50.

45. Georg Wilhelm Friedrich Hegel, *Philosophy of History*, translated by J. Sirbee (New York: P. F. Collier and Son, 1900), 150.

46. Hegel, *Philosophy of History*, 150.

rightfully considered "one of the founders of modern scientific racism, and thus a pioneering theorist of sub-personhood and disrespect."[47] While he argued that humans represent a unified species, he recognized that they were divided into four races, with characteristic differences based on climate. Not surprisingly, Kant considered "the Negro race" the lowest in the human hierarchy. It should be noted, however, that Native Americans, though not classified as one of the four main races, were considered by Kant to be beneath "Negroes." He stated that "this race, too weak for hard labor, too indifferent for diligence, and incapable of any culture, stands—despite the proximity of example and ample encouragement—far below the Negro, who undoubtedly holds the lowest of all remaining levels that we have designated as racial differences."[48]

Kant's "anti-Black" ideology is most clear in his assessment of skin color. For Kant, white was "the ideal skin-color" with all skin colors considered "superior or inferior as they approximate whiteness."[49] He believed that skin color, more than just a matter subject to aesthetic judgment, is an indicator of a person's character and intelligence. In this regard, Blackness indicates a "lazy, soft and dallying" people.[50] With regard to intelligence, Kant's thoughts were made clear in his observations regarding an

47. See Charles W. Mills, *Black Rights/White Wrongs: The Critique of Racial Liberalism* (New York: Oxford University Press, 2017), 31.

48. "On the Use of Teleological Principles in Philosophy," in Jon M. Mikkelsen, *Kant and the Concept of Race: Late Eighteenth-Century Writings* (Albany: State University of New York Press, 2013), 186–87, *Project MUSE,* muse.jhu.edu/book/26503.

49. E. C. Eze, "The Color of Reason: The Idea of 'Race' in Kant's Anthropology," *The Bucknell Review* 38, no. 2 (1995), 200–241 at 217. Retrieved from http://ezproxy.cul.columbia.edu/login?url=https://www-proquest-com.ezproxy. cul.columbia.edu/scholarly-journals/color-reason-idea-race-kants-anthropology/ docview/1289930247/se-2?accountid=10226.

50. "Of the Different Human Races," in Mikkelsen, *Kant and the Concept of Race,* 67.

African male. He said, "This fellow was quite black from head to foot, a clear proof that what he said was stupid."[51] Kant, in fact, supported David Hume's opinion of Black people, as articulated in Hume's infamous footnote in the essay "On National Characteristics." Hume states:

> I am apt to suspect the negroes to be naturally inferior to the whites. There scarcely ever was a civilized nation of that complexion, nor even any individual eminent either in action or speculation. No ingenious manufactures amongst them, no arts, no sciences. On the other hand, the most rude and barbarous of the whites, such as the ancient GERMANS, the present TARTARS, have still something eminent about them, in their valour, form of government, or some other particular. Such a uniform and constant difference could not happen, in so many countries and ages, if nature had not made an original distinction between these breeds of men. Not to mention our colonies, there are NEGROE slaves dispersed all over EUROPE, of whom none ever discovered any symptoms of ingenuity; though low people, without education, will start up amongst us, and distinguish themselves in every profession. In JAMAICA, indeed, they talk of one negroe as a man of parts and learning; but it is likely he is admired for slender accomplishments, like a parrot, who speaks a few words plainly.[52]

Interestingly, again, in the numerous college and post-graduate courses I have taken in which these Enlightenment thinkers were studied, never was their anti-Blackness critically examined, let alone the philosophical foundation that Enlightenment

---

51. Quoted in Eze, "The Color of Reason," 218.

52. David Hume, "On National Character," in *Selected Essays*, edited by Stephen Copely and Andrew Edgar (Oxford University Press, 1993), 360 n120.

thought provided for the flourishing of scientific and religious racism. Most often, the prevalent anti-Black racism of Enlightenment thinkers was ignored.

Both Shakespeare's plays and Enlightenment thought serve as examples of how a narrative of anti-Blackness is so causally, yet effectively, disseminated in society. As uninterrogated and unacknowledged anti-Black tropes are used and disseminated by educational, religious, or other social institutions, a robust anti-Black narrative develops and becomes deeply embedded, even if unwittingly, in the collective psyche and consciousness of a people, leading to a "toxic cultural mindset" regarding Black bodies. To reiterate, it is for this reason that the hymnody of the church which fosters notions of darkness/ blackness as evil is not innocuous. It is the theological precursor to the notion of blackness as an evil threat. This light/dark binary actually projects a worldview in which that which is dark (blackness) must be subjugated, if not overcome by that which is light (whiteness). Simply put, the subtle deployment of these anti-Black precursors and tropes serve as what Isabel Wilkerson describes as "social instructions we receive from childhood."[53] It cannot be emphasized enough that it is through religious and other forms of social discourse that people are socialized into a way of viewing themselves and others; in this instance, a white supremacist/anti-Black way. And, as we will see, this has fatal consequences.

An anti-Black narrative undoubtedly arrived in America with the earliest settlers dispatched from England in 1607 to form what became known as the Jamestown Colony in Virginia. An anti-Black narrative, therefore, was already a part of the cultural soil upon which the first Africans stepped when they disembarked from the *White Lion* ship onto the shores of Point Comfort, Virginia, in 1619. As historian Alden T. Vaughn points out, "the Elizabethan Englishmen's deep-rooted antipathy to

---

53. Wilkerson, *Caste*, 69.

Africans," as documented earlier in this chapter, prevailed in the Virginia colony that these first Africans entered.[54] It mattered little whether they were considered enslaved or indentured. They were Black, and that branded them as inferior beings. Given the African's blackness, to borrow from Ibram Kendi, they were "stamped from the beginning" as sub-human, destined to become chattel. Vaughn notes, "Black men and women brought to Virginia from 1619 to 1629 held from the outset a singularly debased status in the eyes of White Virginians."[55]

With the arrival of the Puritans and Pilgrims, the anti-Black narrative, along with white supremacist assumptions, became constitutive of America's identity—eventually resulting in a moral imaginary in conflict with the very soul of the nation. There is no better evidence of this conflict than the ideological/moral inconsistencies seen in the political leaders who not only reflected but arguably have had the most impact on shaping America's democracy, if not its moral imaginary: Thomas Jefferson and Abraham Lincoln.

Winthrop Jordan says of Thomas Jefferson, "[He] was not a typical nor an ordinary man, but his enormous breadth of interest and his lack of originality make him an effective sounding board for his culture."[56] It is in this way that Thomas Jefferson exemplifies the ideological mindset that shaped the nation and its resultant moral imaginary.

Jefferson, considered the "father" of America's democracy, was the principal architect of the Declaration of Independence. As such, he projected a vision of the nation's soul. "We hold these truths to be self-evident," Jefferson wrote, "that all men are created equal, that they are endowed by their Creator with

---

54. Alden T. Vaughn, *Roots of American Racism: Essays on the Colonial Experience* (Oxford: Oxford University Press, 1995), 129.

55. Vaughn, *Roots of American Racism*, 129.

56. Jordan, *White over Black*, 429.

certain unalienable Rights, that among these are Life, Liberty and the pursuit of Happiness." To be sure, despite this vision, the echoes of his Anglo-Saxon/white chauvinism shone through the Declaration as Jefferson referred to Native Americans as "the merciless Indian Savages, whose known rule of warfare, is an undistinguished destruction of all ages, sexes and conditions." Still, the very enumeration of "unalienable" rights indicates a vision that transcends the "raced" assumptions behind the Declaration itself. What is perhaps most remarkable, as previously stated, is that this vision was even articulated, thereby pointing toward the possibility of a society that would in fact value and respect the sacred dignity of all human beings. Nevertheless, given the "raced" overtones accompanying a vision of equality within the Declaration of Independence, it is not surprising that this vision would be so easily overwhelmed by ideological commitments to "whiteness" as the new nation's government formed itself. It is, however, instructive, for it reveals the nation's defiant resistance to the urgings of its soul and thus its fundamental resolve to be a nation defined not by its "better angels" but by its white supremacist foundation, replete with an anti-Black narrative. Again, this is evinced in Thomas Jefferson.

Jefferson's white supremacist/anti-Black convictions consistently thwarted any vision he may have had of a non-raced America. While he asserted that slavery was a "moral and political depravity,"[57] and "hideous blot"[58] upon the nation, such

---

57. "Thomas Jefferson to Thomas Cooper, 10 September 1814," *Founders Online*, National Archives, https://founders.archives.gov/documents/Jefferson/03-07-02-0471. (Original source: *The Papers of Thomas Jefferson*, Retirement Series, vol. 7, *28 November 1813 to 30 September 1814*, edited by J. Jefferson Looney. [Princeton: Princeton University Press, 2010], 649–55.)

58. Thomas Jefferson to William Short, 8 September 1823," *Founders Online*, National Archives, https://founders.archives.gov/documents/Jefferson/98-01-02-3750. (This is an "Early Access" document from *The Papers of Thomas Jefferson: Retirement Series*. It is not an authoritative final version.)

assertions did not prevent the "father of democracy" from being a savvy slaveholder. The scrupulousness by which he engaged in the slave economy is seen as he carefully notes the value of his Black female chattel. He writes, "I consider labor of a breeding woman as no object, and that a child raised every 2 years is of more profit than the crop of the best laboring men."[59]

Perhaps acting in his mind as a mitigating justification for being an anti-slavery slaveholder was the fact that he viewed Black people as inferior beings who needed white "supervision." Jefferson steadfastly maintained that Blacks were subordinate to whites in all aspects, "body and mind." His oft-quoted "Notes on the State of Virginia" provide ample evidence of his fully formed anti-Black views, complete with sexual tropes. For instance, after making clear the aesthetic difference between Blacks and whites, with particular concern to explain the reason for the dark skin of Black persons, he puts forward his version of Black hypersexuality. He argues that the passion and appearance of Black females renders them so sexually charged that male apes have a "uniform" preference "for the Black woman over [females] of his own species." Jefferson similarly describes the Black male as hypersexualized, stating that Black males "are more ardent after their female; but love seems to be with them more an eager desire, than a tender delicate mixture of sentiment and sensation."[60] Jefferson's view of Black women and men mirrors the anti-Black narrative of the aforementioned European pillagers of Africa who cast Africans as "beastly."

Given his deeply held anti-Black views, Jefferson did not think it possible for Blacks and whites to live together. Conse-

---

59. Jefferson quoted in Cheryl I. Harris, "Whiteness as Property," *Harvard Law Review* 106, no. 8 (June 1993): 1720.

60. Jefferson, *Notes on the State of Virginia* (Philadelphia: Prichard and Hall, 1788).

quently, his anti-slavery views were accompanied by a conviction that free Blacks should be deported from the United States.
The fixed connection between the abolition of slavery and the
colonization of the formerly enslaved is fully voiced in his autobiography. He writes that "Nothing is more certainly written in
the book of fate than that [Black people] are to be free. Nor is it
less certain," he said, "that the two races, equally free, cannot
live in the same government. Nature, habit, opinion has drawn
indelible lines of distinction between them."[61]

In the end, Jefferson's anti-Black, white supremacist views
overrode any incipient vision he may have had for America to
be a place where all people, Black and white, could live and
thrive. It is doubtlessly the case that when he wrote "all men,"
he was not envisioning Black men amongst those "all." While
his democratic vision suggested that slavery was wrong, his
anti-Black predisposition made it impossible for him to affirm
the full humanity of Black people. Hence, his own moral imaginary could not hold a vision of a nation where Black and white
people could co-exist as equals. In this way, Jefferson reflected
the nation's inherent conflict as manifest in a racially delimited
moral imaginary. The same can be said of Abraham Lincoln.

The "Great Emancipator," like Jefferson, at once denounced
slavery and Black equality. While political practicalities prevented Lincoln from being a "radical" abolitionist, thereby advocating for the immediate abolition of slavery, his moral
disregard for slavery was deep. It was not unusual for him to
speak against the institution even when this threatened his own
political ambitions. Such was the case when, as a member of the
General Assembly in Illinois, twenty-six-year-old Lincoln voted
"No" to a resolution to ban abolitionist societies within the state.
In so doing he proclaimed: "The institution of slavery is
founded on both injustice and bad policy." This vote accorded

---

61. *The Autobiography of Thomas Jefferson 1743–1790*, Kindle edition, 48.

with his later stated belief that "if slavery is not wrong, nothing is wrong."[62]

It would be in his 1854 Peoria, Illinois, speech to lobby against the passage of the Kansas-Nebraska Act and for retaining the Missouri Compromise that Lincoln's anti-slavery position as well as his views regarding Black inequality would begin to come into clear view. In this speech, Lincoln stressed his personal disdain for slavery, calling it a "monstrous injustice." His disdain notwithstanding, however, he recognized the impracticality of slavery's immediate abolition. He advocates for its gradual end.

Nevertheless, always the pragmatic politician concerned with the preservation of the Union, he accepted slavery in the territories where it already existed as long as it was not extended into those territories where it did not. This position, he said, corresponded with what the Framers of the Constitution intended and protected the integrity of the Missouri Compromise. Given the Constitution's Fugitive Slave Clause, Lincoln was not incorrect in assuming that the Framers of the Constitution accepted the institution of slavery and did not question slaveholding states' jurisdiction over those who were enslaved. Frederick Douglass captured Lincoln's position well in a speech at the unveiling of a monument to Lincoln. Douglass said of Lincoln:

> He came into the Presidential chair upon one principle alone, namely, opposition to the extension of slavery. His arguments in furtherance of this policy had their motive and mainspring in his patriotic devotion to the interests of his own race. To protect, defend, and perpetuate slavery in the States where it existed Abraham Lincoln was not less ready than any other President to draw the sword of the nation. He was ready to execute all the supposed constitutional guarantees of the United

---

62. This rendering of the episode in Lincoln's career is redacted from Doris Kearns Goodwin's reporting of it in *Leadership in Turbulent Times* (New York: Simon and Schuster, 2018), 17.

States Constitution in favor of the slave system anywhere inside the slave States. He was willing to pursue, recapture, and send back the fugitive slave to his master, and to suppress a slave rising for liberty.[63]

It was as Lincoln pondered the real possibilities of emancipating the enslaved that the conflict between his "better angels" and his white supremacist/anti-Black predisposition clearly emerged. As he admitted to being at a loss for how to effectively eradicate slavery, he conceded that he was at an even greater loss about what to do with emancipated slaves. His solution, like Jefferson's, was to dispatch free Black people to another country. It is in this argument that we see his belief in Black inferiority, and thus the extent of his inner conflict—and indeed, the inherent conflict within the nation itself.

For Lincoln it was a conflict between his faith and his sense of white superiority. This personal conflict mirrored the conflict between the Declaration of Independence's vision and the Constitution's whiteness. Lincoln spoke to both as he said on the one hand:

> If the negro is a man, why then my ancient faith teaches me that "all men are created equal;" and that there can be no moral right in connection with one man's making a slave of another....I say this is the leading principle—the sheet anchor of American republicanism. Our Declaration of Independence says: "We hold these truths to be self-evident; that all men are created equal; that they are endowed by their Creator with certain inalienable rights; that among these are life, liberty and the pursuit of happiness. That to secure these rights, governments are instituted among men, DERIVING THEIR JUST POWERS FROM THE CONSENT OF THE GOVERNED."

---

63. Oration by Frederick Douglass Delivered on the Occasion of the Unveiling of the Freedmen's Monument, April 14, 1876, 5, Anacostia Community Museum Archives, https://edan.si.edu/transcription/pdf_files/12955.pdf.

And on the other hand:

> If all earthly power were given me, I should not know what
> to do, as to the existing institution. My first impulse would be
> to free all the slaves, and send them to Liberia,—to their own
> native land. But a moment's reflection would convince me,
> that whatever of high hope, (as I think there is) there may be
> in this, in the long run, its sudden execution is impossible....
>
> What next? Free them, and make them politically and so-
> cially, our equals? My own feelings will not admit of this; and
> if mine would, we well know that those of the great mass of
> white people will not.
>
> We cannot, then, make them equals.[64]

While Lincoln is firm in his conviction that Black people are
not equal to whites, it is important to note that in Lincoln we do
not see—as was the case in Jefferson—the strong influence of a
developed anti-Black narrative with the tropes of Black people
as bestial and sub-human. Thus, in his Peoria Speech he ab-
solutely rejects the notion that there is "no difference between
hogs and negroes." He declares that "there is humanity in the
negro."[65]

In the final analysis, while Lincoln recognized the rights
promoted in the Declaration of Independence for all men, even
Black men, to govern themselves, he still could not admit Black
men to be equal to whites. Therefore, Lincoln argued for a subtle
distinction between "inalienable rights" and political and social
rights. Inalienable rights, he claimed, afford individuals the
right to be free and to have the benefits of their own labor.
Hence, the Declaration itself served, in Lincoln's mind, as an
anti-slavery document.

---

64. Peoria Speech, October 16, 1854, Lincoln Home National Historic Site
Illinois, https://www.nps.gov/liho/learn/historyculture/peoriaspeech.htm.

65. Peoria Speech.

However, it did not speak to political and social rights. Political rights are those such as the right to the vote and to serve on juries. Social rights would imply the right to interact with whites equally in public spaces and—most unacceptably—to enter into interracial marriage. For Lincoln, "natural rights were one thing, political and social rights were quite another."[66] Making this distinction enabled Lincoln to maintain his opposition to slavery while not betraying the common prejudices of his day—and perhaps his own white prejudices that Blacks were not equals to whites.

Nevertheless, in harboring this belief in white superiority and Black inferiority, he effectively betrayed not only the Declaration's vision but also his stated "ancient faith." Lincoln's attempt to resolve his inner conflict and perhaps mitigate the dual betrayal led him to support Black colonization: conceding the Black man's right to self-governance, hence to "inalienable rights," but in a land away from white people. Historian Eric Foner aptly captures Lincoln's position when he says that, for Lincoln, "Blacks might be entitled to the natural rights of mankind, but ultimately they should enjoy them outside of the United States."[67]

Lincoln's inability to see Black people as equal to whites is even more pronounced in his objection to the way in which the Constitution's Three-Fifths Clause disadvantages white people in non-slaveholding states in relation to whites in slave-holding states. He argues,

> Five slaves are counted as being equal to three whites. The slaves do not vote; they are only counted and so used, as to swell the influence of the white people's votes [in the slave-holding states]. . . .

---

66. Eric Foner, *The Fiery Trial: Abraham Lincoln and American Slavery* (New York: W. W. Norton and Company Inc., 2010), Kindle edition, 110. See his discussion of Lincoln's developing views on this issue.

67. Foner, *The Fiery Trial*, 97.

Thus each white man in South Carolina is more than the double of any man in Maine. This is all because South Carolina, besides her free people, has 384,984 slaves. The South Carolinian has precisely the same advantage over the white man in every other free State, as well as in Maine. He is more than the double of any one of us in this crowd. The same advantage, but not to the same extent, is held by all the citizens of the slave States, over those of the free....

I insist, that whether I shall be a whole man, or only, the half of one, in comparison with others, is a question in which I am somewhat concerned.[68]

Ever evident in Lincoln's argument is the ease with which his sense of white superiority overcomes any moral conviction he holds about human equality. While he argues that the consequence of the constitutional concession to slavery means that all white men are not counted as equal to one another, he expresses no disagreement with the constitutional proclamation that a Black person is considered three-fifths of a person in relationship to whites. Acceptance of the Three-Fifths Clause seems to belie his affirmation of Black humanity.

Once again, Lincoln's argument points to the Constitution's fundamental commitment to white supremacy despite the Declaration's vision of "inalienable" equality.

In the end, Lincoln's own "moral and ideological dilemma" actually reflected an enduring conflict between the nation's soul and its white supremacist foundation. Just as an "underlying emotional commitment to whiteness and white supremacy" prevented Lincoln from being able to imagine a nation where white people and Black people could live as equals, this same commitment has prevented the nation from being a place where Black people are treated justly.[69] Such a nation is beyond the

---

68. Peoria Speech.

69. George M. Fredrickson, "A Man but Not a Brother: Abraham Lincoln

realm of a moral imaginary defined by whiteness. In speaking the truth about Lincoln, Frederick Douglass spoke a truth about the nation as well. He said,

> Abraham Lincoln was not, in the fullest sense of the word, either our man or our model. In his interests, in his associations, in his habits of thought, and in his prejudices, he was a white man. He was pre-eminently the white man's President, entirely devoted to the welfare of white men.[70]

This country's white supremacist basis and concomitant anti-Black character have prevented it from becoming a nation where Black people's full humanity is valued. The fact that this has continued to be the norm—one that has been expressed from the highest office in the land, and well beyond the nation's formative years—suggests again the way in which anti-Black white supremacy has taken hold of the nation's moral imaginary. There is no better exemplar of this in the twentieth century than the nation's twenty-eighth president, Woodrow Wilson.

As the first southerner elected president after Reconstruction, Wilson was determined to reassert the white supremacist/anti-Black values of the defeated slavocracy. He defied the Reconstruction amendments that gestured toward Black equality. Essentially, Wilson seemed resolved to reinstate, for all intents and purposes, the Constitution's Three-Fifths Clause. So, even as he proclaimed World War I as the war to "make the world safe for democracy," his actions made clear that it was a democracy reserved for whites only. Not long after he assumed the presidency, Wilson began to roll back Black economic gains and oversaw aggressive resegregation of agencies within the federal government. Most appalling, he allowed for the institution

---

and Racial Equality," *The Journal of Southern History* 41, no. 1 (1975): 39–58 at 53, 47, JSTOR, www.jstor.org/stable/2206706.

70. Douglass, *Oration*, 4–5.

of Jim Crow indignities, such as segregated dining and separate restrooms, within federal buildings. The support of Jim Crow policies from a president who received significant backing from the Black electorate, to whom he had made promises to advance civil rights, drew the ire of prominent civil rights leaders like William Trotter.

Securing an Oval Office meeting with Wilson in 1914, Trotter came with a prepared statement listing his grievances and noting the sense of betrayal felt by the Black community and its leaders. Wilson rebuffed Trotter's criticisms, claiming that his segregationist policies were in the best interest of Black people as these policies "were seeking, not to put the Negro employees at a disadvantage but...to make arrangements which would prevent any kind of friction between the white employees and the Negro employees."[71] Wilson's explanation virtually repeated the logic he used while he was president of Princeton University when he justified the lack of Black applicants, as if to hide the fact that he actually discouraged Black admissions. He said then, "The whole temper and tradition of the place [Princeton] are such that no Negro has ever applied for admission, and it seems unlikely that the question will ever assume practical form."[72]

Moreover, his segregationist defense echoed the sentiments of earlier abolitionist whites, like Lincoln, who proclaimed that Black people would be better served by removal from the country, given "unsurmountable white prejudices" regarding Black equality.[73]

---

71. The recounting of this incident as well as quotes rely on the story as told in Dick Lehr, "The Racist Legacy of Woodrow Wilson," *The Atlantic*, November 27, 2018, https://www.theatlantic.com/politics/archive/2015/ 11/wilson-legacy-racism/417549/.

72. Quoted in "Princeton's Problem: President Woodrow Wilson's 'Racist' Legacy," https://www.nj.com/mercer/2015/11/woodrow_wilsons_racism_at_center_of_princeton_u_st.html.

73. Fredrickson, "A Man but Not a Brother," 48.

Incredulous at Wilson's response, Trotter retorted, "Have you a 'New Freedom' for white Americans and a new slavery for your Afro-American fellow citizens? God forbid!"

Incensed by Trotter's "attitude" Wilson threw him out of the Oval Office.[74] Wilson's outrage was no doubt fueled not simply by what he regarded as disrespect shown to the president, but more so by the fact that it was a Black man who had dared to speak to a white man in such a manner. That Trotter confronted Wilson as an equal, if not with an air of righteous superiority, inflamed Wilson's well-established white supremacist beliefs.

If his time as president at Princeton, or even as governor of New Jersey, did not clearly evince his bigotry, a five-volume history of America which he authored certainly did. In his treatment of American history, Wilson portrayed the Reconstruction as a dismal period that imposed upon southern whites "the intolerable burden of governments sustained by the votes of ignorant negroes."[75] In his re-telling of history, he also made very clear his profound anti-Black beliefs. In so doing, he actually presaged one of the most audaciously blatant displays of anti-Blackness to take place in the White House up to that time: a White House screening of D. W. Griffith's *The Birth of a Nation*.

This 1915 film, based on the book *The Clansman* by Wilson's former Johns Hopkins classmate Thomas Dixon, presented the Ku Klux Klan as heroes and Black people as ignorant, uncivilized animals. The film employed the vilest and most vicious anti-Black tropes. Most notably, Black men were portrayed as rapacious brutes with white women as their prized prey. This film was screened in the East Room of the White House on February 18, 1915.[76] As if to make clear

---

74. Lehr, "The Racist Legacy of Woodrow Wilson."

75. Woodrow Wilson, *A History of the American People—In Five Volumes*, vol. 5, *Reunion and Nationalization* (1901; New York: Cosmos Inc., 2008), 58.

76. For more on the details of the screening and what led up to it as well as controversies following it, see Mark E. Benbow, "Birth of a Quotation:

Wilson's anti-Black commitments and his support of the film, statements from his aforementioned history volumes were quoted (even if taken out of context, as some claim) on note-cards throughout the film.[77] One of the most notable quotations championed the emergence of the Klan. It read, "The white men of the South were aroused by a mere instinct of self-preservation...until at last there had sprung into existence a great Ku Klux Klan, a veritable empire of the South to protect the Southern country."[78]

Even though the early twentieth century was considered the "nadir" of post–Civil War race relations in the United States, Woodrow Wilson's white supremacist/anti-Black convictions are viewed by some as exceptionally vile even by the standards of that time. Whether such an assessment is accurate, Wilson's convictions certainly reflected fundamental attitudes in the na-tion. It should be noted that the evening after the White House screening of *The Birth of a Nation* it was also screened at the Na-tional Press Club with Supreme Court justices, including the Chief Justice of the Supreme Court, along with thirty-eight sen-ators and fifty representatives in attendance.[79]

Suffice it to say that the fact that the nation could twice elect a man who openly expressed such despicable anti-Black racism revealed the troubled state of the nation's moral imaginary. But if Woodrow Wilson was emblematic of the nation's white su-premacist/anti-Blackness in the twentieth century, the 2016 elec-tion of Donald Trump set the standard for the same in the twenty-first.

Woodrow Wilson and 'Like Writing History with Lightning,'" *The Journal of the Gilded Age and Progressive Era* 9, no. 4 (2010): 509–33, JSTOR, www.jstor.org/stable/20799409.

77. See Benbow, "Birth of a Quotation."

78. Dylan Matthews, "Woodrow Wilson Was Extremely Racist—Even by the Standards of His Time," https://www.vox.com/policy-and-politics/ 2015/ 11/20/9766896/woodrow-wilson-racist; Benbow, "Birth of a Quotation," 517.

79. Benbow, "Birth of a Quotation," 514–15.

From the moment Trump first announced his campaign mantra to "Make America Great Again," Black America in general had a visceral reaction. Judging from my own barbershop and church conversations, as well as those with family, friends, and colleagues, Black people instinctively knew that "great" was a euphemism for "white." The only question was to what particular period in America's history of virulent displays of "whiteness" Trump was advocating a return. Nevertheless, Black people's instincts regarding the slogan were quickly proved correct as Trump shamelessly trafficked in white supremacist and anti-Black rhetoric throughout the campaign. In so doing, he tapped into white America's deep-seated, white racist fears about people of color, beginning with his opening warnings about Mexican immigrants: "When Mexico sends its people, they're not sending their best.... They're bringing drugs. They're bringing crime," he said. "They're rapists. And some, I assume, are good people."[80] His white racist attacks on Mexicans continued into his presidency.[81]

Trump was even more shameless in his not-so-subtle evocation of an anti-Black narrative as he advanced tropes of threatening Blackness. Throughout his 2016 campaign he consistently portrayed Black communities as virtual enclaves of omnipresent danger and overwhelming violence. He said of them, "You can't walk out the street, you buy a loaf of bread and you end up getting shot."[82] He continued these tropes during his 2020 campaign for re-election. In fact, he dug even deeper into them as he

---

80. Katie Reilly, "Here Are All the Times Donald Trump Insulted Mexico," *TIME*, August 31, 2016, https://time.com/4473972/donald-trump-mexico-meeting-insult/.

81. Z. Byron Wolf, "Trump Basically Called Mexicans Rapists Again," CNN, April 6, 2018, https://www.cnn.com/ 2018/04/06/politics/trump-mexico-rapists.

82. Jeremy Diamond, "Trump Refers to 'Ghettos' in Discussing African-American Issues," CNN, October 27, 2016, https://www.cnn.com/2016/10/27/politics/donald-trump-ghettos-african-americans/ index.html.

touted his roll-back of President Obama's anti-discrimination housing policies. Trump said these roll-backs were necessary in order to protect white suburban housewives from the violence of inner cities.[83] These claims were tantamount to Wilson's White House screening of *The Birth of a Nation*, with its scene of a rampaging Black man attempting to rape a white woman.

That Trump's campaign to "Make America Great Again" was defined by such blatant white supremacist/anti-Black convictions was unsurprising given that he rose to "political prominence by peddling the racist myth that [President Obama] was not American."[84] The suggestion that the first Black president was not a real American tapped into America's white supremacist foundation that America was intended first and foremost to be a white nation. Moreover, Trump's persistent claim that Obama was born in Kenya was a brazen nod to the anti-Black caricature of Africans as wild, uncivilized beasts—unsuited for white society, and so all the more unsuited to the office of President of the "great/white" nation. The allegation that an African Black man was usurping the Oval Office served as an obvious "dog-whistle" to white America, reinforcing the urgent call to "Make America Great Again."

The juxtaposition of a presidential candidate campaigning on racial fear and lies to succeed the nation's first Black president starkly reveals the nation's inherent conflict between its white supremacist/anti-Black foundation and the vision of its better angels. What happened on November 9, 2016, laid bare once again America's stubborn resistance to the urgings of its

---

83. John Fritze, David Jackson, and Michael Collins, "Critics Slam Trump 'Suburban Housewife' Tweet as Racist, Sexist 'Dog Scream' Play for White Voters," *USA Today*, August 12, 2020, https://www.usatoday.com/story/news/politics/elections/2020/08/12/trump-critics-see-tweet-the-suburban-housewife-sexist-racist/.

84. Ta-Nehisi Coates, "My President Was Black," *The Atlantic*, January/February 2017, https://www.theatlantic.com/magazine/archive/2017/01/my-president-was.../508793/.

soul, thus revealing America's troubled moral imaginary. Clarified once more was the fact that the nation's "raced" moral imaginary is unable to hold a vision of a society in which there is equal justice for people of color, most notably Black people. As Joseph Ellis, a Pulitzer Prize-winning historian, thus rightly pointed out, "Anybody who says that the [2016] election is not, at least in part [or, as I would suggest, in large part], a racial event is functioning as an apologist, whether they know it or not, for white prejudice."[85] Indeed, in the aftermath of the election to "Make America Great Again" two things became abundantly clear: not only the deadly combination of white supremacist values and an anti-Black narrative but also the profound impact of that combination on the nation's moral imaginary. This is evidenced by the fact that, with little provocation, dehumanizing and sometimes deadly attacks were unleashed on Black bodies, typically with impunity, attacks representing some of the most racially charged episodes in the nation's history. To this we will now turn.

Making America Great Again and the Matter of Black Lives

The "Make America Great Again" vision brought to the surface the nation's fundamental white supremacist values as defined by an anti-Black narrative. It bears repeating that within the anti-Black narrative, the Black body is seen as dangerously threatening. Like animals, Black people are viewed as likely to erupt into life-threatening tirades with little provocation, and thus are inherently violent and to be feared. President Trump's pledge to "Make America Great Again" played upon this fear, provoking in white America an almost reflexive response to

---

85. Quoted in John Blake and Tawanda Scott Sambou, "How Trump's Victory Turns into Another 'Lost Cause,'" CNN, December 28, 2016, http://www.cnn.com/2016/12/28/us/lost-cause-trump/index.html.

protect "whiteness" against the "perceived" threat of Blackness at any cost. This is seen in the prevalence of anti-Black incidents across the country during Trump's presidency.

Almost routinely, Black people are subjected to incidents in which individuals, some of whom might otherwise consider themselves "non-racist," instinctively call the police because they feel somehow threatened by a Black person engaging in ordinary human endeavors. Such an incident happened to a Black Yale student Lolade Siyonbola, who was napping on a couch in one of her dormitory's common spaces, as was the habit of other students.[86] Similarly, Amanda Gorman, the nation's first youth poet laureate, after delivering the inaugural poem during the swearing in of President Biden and Vice President Harris, was deemed "suspicious" by a security guard who "tailed" her as she walked to her home. As Gorman rightly pointed out, "This is the reality of Black girls: One day you're called an icon, the next day, a threat."[87]

These incidents suggest that the reality of a Black person simply going about the business of being human in a society teeming with a dehumanizing anti-Black narrative means that something must be wrong and danger awaits. And so, police have been called on Black people waiting, barbequing, or birdwatching. Even worse is when the presence of a Black body almost instinctively elicits deadly force from police.

Research makes clear, for instance, that Black males are two-and-a-half times more likely to be killed by police than white males.[88] Other studies reveal that a Black person fatally shot by

---

86. Scott Jaschik, "Yale Police Called on Black Student Taking a Nap," *Inside Higher Ed*, May 10, 2018, https://www.insidehighered.com/news/2018/05/10/yale-police-called-black-graduate-student-who-was-napping.

87. Kelly Murray and Alta Spells, "Amanda Gorman, Inaugural Poet, 'Tailed' by Security Guard on Her Walk Home," CNN, March 6, 2021, https://www.cnn.com/2021/03/06/us/amanda-gorman-followed-security-guard-trnd/index.html.

88. Frank Edwards, Hedwig Lee, Michael Esposito, "Risk of Being Killed by Police Use of Force in the United States by Age, Race–Ethnicity,

police is twice as likely to be unarmed as a white person. These findings reflect bad police techniques, and systemic racism within law enforcement agencies, but the problem goes beyond these things.[89] The influence of an anti-Black narrative is apparent in a study that concluded that "Black faces looked more criminal to police officers; the more Black the more criminal." Furthermore, the study found that "Black faces and Black bodies can trigger thoughts of crime [and] thinking of crime can trigger thoughts of Black people."[90] These studies help explain why Black people make up 24 percent of fatal police encounters, despite the fact that Black people make up only 13 percent of the general population.[91] The plain truth is that Black encounters with police are more deadly due in no small part to the influence of an anti-Black narrative.

And so it was that nineteen-year-old Elijah McClain in Aurora, Colorado, was described by a caller as "sketchy," thus causing the police to interrupt his walk home from a convenience store where he had purchased an iced tea. Ironically, Elijah tried to disrupt the anti-Black narrative by telling the police that he was an "introvert," just different. "I don't do drugs," he said, "I don't even kill flies." He was essentially trying to reclaim his humanity from an anti-Black narrative that had rendered him in the police's mind a dangerous beast ready to

---

and Sex," *Proceedings of the National Academy of Sciences* 116, no. 34 (August 20, 2019): 16793–16798; DOI: 10.1073/pnas.1821204116, https://www.pnas.org/content/116/34/16793.

89. Lynne Peeples, "What the Data Say about Police Brutality and Racial Bias—and Which Reforms Might Work," *Nature*, June 19, 2020, https://www.nature.com/articles/d41586-020-01846-z#ref-CR2.

90. Jennifer L. Eberhardt, Phillip Atiba Goff, Valerie J. Purdie, "Seeing Black: Race, Crime, and Visual Processing," *Journal of Personality and Social Psychology* 87, no. 6 (2004): 876–93, https://web.stanford.edu/group/scspi/media/_media/working_papers/_archive/eberhardt_jennifer_wp_20070330b.pdf.

91. See "Police Violence Map, Mapping Police Violence," https://mappingpoliceviolence.org/ [https://perma.cc/9T9B-9MWQ].

erupt. Unfortunately, Elijah's pleadings were not able to override the narrative deeply implanted within the consciousness of the officers. As a consequence, they subdued Elijah with a carotid hold, cutting off blood flow to his brain. When paramedics arrived on the scene, they administered ketamine, a strong sedative, to the unarmed, 140-pound already-handcuffed McClain. McClain went into cardiac arrest on the way to the hospital and eventually died.

It was this same anti-Black narrative that made it seem necessary to shackle a paralyzed Jacob Blake to his hospital bed. Jacob had been paralyzed from the waist down after being shot seven times in the back, in front of his children, as he tried to get into his car. This life-altering event occurred during an encounter with the police in Kenosha, Wisconsin.[92] Ironically, the discriminatory effect of the anti-Black narrative played out in reverse in Kenosha during protests over Jacob Blake's shooting. It played out as police allowed a visibly and heavily armed seventeen-year-old white male, who had just killed two people, to walk away without incident, apparently even offering him water at one point.[93] Befitting the promulgator of the call to "Make America Great Again," President Trump defended the actions of this white teenager and even suggested that members of his administration do the same.[94]

---

92. For more on this incident, see Christina Morales, "What We Know About the Shooting of Jacob Blake," *New York Times*, March 26, 2021, https://www.nytimes.com/article/jacob-blake-shooting-kenosha.html.

93. Joyce Sohyun Lee, Robert O'Harrow Jr., and Elyse Samuels, "Kenosha: How Two Men's Paths Crossed in an Encounter That Has Divided the Nation," *Washington Post*, November 19, 2020, https://www.washingtonpost.com/investigations/2020/11/19/kenosha-shooting-kyle-rittenhouse-interview/?arc404=true.

94. Julia Ainsley, "Internal Document Shows Trump Officials Were Told to Make Comments Sympathetic to Kyle Rittenhouse," NBC News, October 1, 2020, https://www.nbcnews.com/politics/national-security/internal-document-shows-trump-officials-were-told-make-comments-sympathetic-n1241581.

When people suggest that "bad cops" are not indicative of all cops, it is instructive to remember how pervasive the anti-Black narrative is: law enforcement officers do not need to be corrupt or overtly racist to see Black bodies through a lens of threat, fear, and criminality. The police are a part of the same public that is "socialized" into an anti-Black narrative. So, as with those who instinctively call police on Black people going about life activities, such is the case with many of the deadly encounters between Black people and police. Both indicate the influence of anti-Blackness on the moral imaginary.

The absurdity of the anti-Black narrative for Black bodies, as well as its profound impact on the country's moral imaginary, has been laid bare during the COVID-19 pandemic. When the scientific and medical community made clear that wearing a mask could help mitigate the spread of the virus, several states ordered mask mandates. At least two states recognized the anti-Black responses that white people might have in seeing Black people in masks. Then, instead of addressing the problematic nature of such responses, responsibility was placed on Black people to avoid eliciting fear from the white public. For instance, in initially issuing its mask mandate, Franklin County, Ohio's Health Department also warned Black people to wear "brightly colored" masks and to avoid masks with "gang symbolisms" or masks that could "elicit deeply held stereotypes."[95] Officials in Oregon's Lincoln County also initially exempted its Black and Latinx population from wearing masks for fear of racial profiling.[96]

---

95. Meagan Flynn, "Ohio County Apologizes for 'Offensive' Guide Urging Minorities to Avoid 'Gang Symbolism' on Masks," *Washington Post*, May 22, 2020, https://www.washingtonpost.com/nation/2020/05/22/face-masks-african-americans-ohio/.

96. Joseph Guzman, "A County in Oregon Is Exempting People of Color from Mask Requirement Due to Racial Profiling," *The Hill*, June 24, 2020, https://thehill.com/changing-america/respect/equality/504362-a-county-in-oregon-is-exempting-people-of-color-from-mask.

Unfortunately, Black people—especially Black men—have had to weigh the risks of being exposed to COVID-19 against being seen as an even more dangerous threat because they were wearing masks. Several incidents were reported in which Black males were met with suspicion because they were following COVID protocols and wearing masks in public spaces. As one study reported, "Many Black men...have voiced on social media their dual concerns over their bodily safety: either from disease, by virtue of not wearing a mask, or from the police, by virtue of wearing one. As educator Aaron Thomas tweeted, "I want to stay alive but I also want to stay alive."[97]

That Black people are disproportionately impacted by COVID-19 has further revealed not only the violently lethal nature of the anti-Black narrative but also how it has become an acceptable part of society. One study succinctly described the intersecting realities of an anti-Black narrative and COVID-19 as it reported:

> Systemic racism multiplied chances for contracting COVID-19 at seemingly every turn and worsened outcomes for those with the disease. Black employees were less likely to have jobs that mobilized for remote work, and instead were disproportionately called into essential jobs at grocery stores or as home health assistants. The absence of benefits or sick leave at many of these jobs incentivized some to continue attending work, even in these dangerous conditions, to stave off eviction or starvation. Black people were also more likely to face unstable housing situations or live in communities with poor access to health care, making it harder to effectively self-isolate or access

---

97. Caroline V. Lawrence and the COVID-Dynamic Team, "Masking Up: A COVID-19 Face-Off between Anti-Mask Laws and Mandatory Mask Orders for Black Americans," *California Law Review* (November 2020), https://www.californialawreview.org/display-author/caroline-v-lawrence-the-covid-dynamic-team/.

treatment. Moreover, they faced the risk of not being taken seriously by doctors when they presented with symptoms.[98]

Essentially, the fact that Black people are disproportionately trapped in poverty, with its social co-morbidities of inadequate health care, substandard housing, and insufficient employment and educational and recreational opportunities, is the result of an uninterrupted anti-Black narrative. When we think of Black people's vulnerability to COVID-19 and the danger imposed upon them for wearing masks in order to prevent falling victim to the virus, ReNika Moore of the ACLU's Racial Justice Program was right when she said, "It's a 'lose-lose' scenario."[99] COVID-19 has revealed the everyday conundrum the anti-Black narrative imposes upon Black existence. Black people must face every day a Hobson's choice between "death and dying."

There is no getting around it: an anti-Black narrative is pervasive in America's social-cultural mindset. The narrative has so impacted the nation's moral imaginary that "letting Black people die" has virtually become an acceptable part of the nation's day-to-day reality. This is the cumulative consequence of not acknowledging and interrogating the narrative when it is deployed within our educational and religious institutions. When the anti-Black narrative is left uninterrupted to interact with the likewise unacknowledged white supremacist ideology, the result is that deadly assaults upon Black bodies become inevitable, whether from the living conditions in which they are trapped or from encounters by citizens with the police. And so now, what does this really mean for the matter of Black lives in this country?

---

98. See Lawrence and the COVID-Dynamic Team, "Masking Up."

99. Scottie Andrew, "An Oregon County Drops Its Mask Exemption for People of Color after Racist Response," CNN, June 25, 2020, https://www.cnn.com/2020/06/24/us/oregon-county-people-of-color-mask-trnd/index.html.

An Ongoing Conversation

In summary, what this chapter has shown is that a long-established narrative of anti-Blackness, interacting with the nation's white supremacist foundation, has overwhelmed the soul of this nation and impacted its moral imaginary in such a way that perilous realities for Black lives are virtually normalized. To be sure, not until an anti-Black narrative is effectively confronted will Black lives ever really matter in this nation. It is no wonder, then, that the instinctive response to Black injustice is not that "Black lives matter," but that "all lives matter." The nation's moral imaginary simply cannot hold a vision in which Black lives matter as much as white lives, let alone serve as the symbolic representation for all lives, and thus what it means to be human.

"So, what are we to do now?" my son asked in response to the police slaying of Philando Castile in 2016. He asked this same question four years later after watching the police fire seven shots into the back of Jacob Blake. With the repetition of his question I felt that "powerlessness" that James Baldwin aptly describes as the feeling of every Black parent at some point in time. It is the feeling that "no matter *what* you do, you are powerless, you are really powerless, against the force of the world that is out to tell your child that he has no right to be alive. And no amount of liberal jargon, and no amount of talk about how well and how far we have progressed, does anything to soften or to point out any solution to this dilemma."[100]

As much as Baldwin's words captured my feelings when confronted by my son's question, I did not want to give myself over to that sense of powerlessness. After all, I am an Episcopal

---

100. James Baldwin, "The Uses of the Blues," in *The Cross of Redemption: Uncollected Writings*, edited with introduction by Randall Kenan (New York: Pantheon Books, 2010), Kindle edition, 73.

priest and theologian. I believe in God's promise of a just future. Yet that promise seemed meaningless as young Black lives continued to be lost to the seemingly intractable narrative of anti-Blackness, not to speak of the Black lives being lost to Covid-19 at a rate more than two-and-a-half times that of white lives lost.[101] I was not sure if my faith could stand up to the weight of these realities, let alone to the gravity of my son's question. Nevertheless, I was not quite ready to give it over to the reality of anti-Blackness. I was determined not to let the violence of anti-Black white supremacy take my faith in the same way as it was taking Black lives. And so, literally clinging to faith in the justice of God, I continued the conversations with my son.

---

101. Data reflects deaths up to December 10, 2020. The only group that has experienced more deaths than Black Americans has been Indigenous Americans. Black, Indigenous and Latino Americans all have COVID-19 death rates more than 2.7 times those of white Americans, who experience the lowest age-adjusted rates. See "The Color of Coronavirus: Covid-19 Deaths by Race and Ethnicity in the U.S.," https://www.apmresearchlab.org/covid/deaths-by-race.

2

More Than Just Monuments

*"He [Trump] literally is reigniting the KKK.... Supporting
these confederate statues is really about the same thing as
supporting the KKK—white supremacy. How come white
people can't see that?"*

This was a text I received from my son as part of a text conversation concerning President Trump's refusal to consider renaming the ten military bases named for Confederate soldiers. After noting the absurdity of military bases named for those who actually fought against the country, my son went on to discuss the way in which Confederate monuments, which President Trump vociferously supported, foster violence against Black lives.

I do not remember seeing Confederate monuments while I was growing up in Dayton, Ohio. I would later learn that there are only five of them in Ohio, most in cemeteries where Confederate soldiers are buried.[1] This accounts for why Confederate monuments are not a part of my childhood memories. However,

---

1. Chris Stewart, "Debate, Passions Flare in South as Statues, Symbols of Confederacy Come Down in New Orleans," *Dayton Daily News,* June 24, 2020, https://www.daytondailynews.com/news/confederate-monuments-ohio-yes-surprisingly-here-are-few/rsAByJ0LbODRrI6eEsdJRO/.

what I do remember from my childhood are Confederate flags. Most often I saw them waving on the back of trucks or as custom designs on license plates. Occasionally, on drives through parts of rural Ohio, I saw Confederate flags flying from flagpoles on people's homes or in their yards.

My body still holds the memory of the feelings I would get anytime I encountered these flags. They were feelings of dread and fear. They were reinforced by my father's remark, whenever we came upon these flags: "Don't think we're supposed to be here."

The dread and fear that Confederate flags ignited in me during my childhood have continued into adulthood. Consequently, when I encounter Confederate flags flying from trucks while I am driving, I do all that I can to get them out of my line of vision, even to the point of pulling over on the side of the road until the vehicle with the offending flag is out of sight.

I will never forget driving from Birmingham to Montgomery, Alabama, along I-65 when I passed a huge Confederate flag flying alongside the highway. I had heard about this flag, dedicated amidst much controversy by the Sons of Confederate Veterans in 2005. But hearing about it and seeing it were two different things. As I approached it, looming so large that one cannot fail to see it, my heart began to race. I felt myself growing anxious. I began questioning my decision to make this drive by myself, even in daylight hours. By the time I reached my destination in Montgomery, I was still feeling unsettled. My uneasiness grew as I noticed Confederate flags flying throughout the city. Needless to say, during my time in Montgomery with a group of students and church leaders from New York, I skipped my typical morning jogs outdoors. The wisdom of my decision not to wander about Montgomery alone was further confirmed when I saw the large monument to Confederate soldiers on the grounds of the state capital.

My encounter with Confederate monuments filled me with the same sense of dread and fear as did Confederate flags.

Needless to say, unable to avoid walking past Montgomery's monument every day, I literally counted the days until I could leave the city. After I left, I thought about Black communities throughout the South where such monuments are a part of the city landscape. I simply cannot imagine having to navigate daily life unable to avoid running into these monuments to men who committed treason in an effort to protect white supremacy and to keep people like me in slavery.

Those feelings came back to me when I read my son's short text connecting support of Confederate monuments with the rise of the Ku Klux Klan. He had rightly pointed to the historical relationship between the erection of these monuments and the rise of white supremacist fervor, and he was recognizing the fear they both evoke in Black people. Others understand that connection as well. So it came as no surprise that Trump, having campaigned on the promise to "Make America Great Again," would come to the defense of the monuments. "Sad to see the history and culture of our great country being ripped apart with the removal of our beautiful statues and monuments," he tweeted.[2]

Make no mistake about it: Confederate memorials on the public square are about more than "beautiful statutes and monuments." In truth, they signal the conflict between the nation's white supremacist foundation and its soul. This chapter will therefore explore the historic and symbolic significance of these Confederate monuments, the better to appreciate their implications for the nation's moral imaginary.

The History They Tell

Since the August 2017 "Unite the Right Rally" in Charlottesville, Virginia—ostensibly organized to protest the removal of a statue

---

2. President Donald Trump, tweet, August 17, 2017, 9:07 a.m.

memorializing Robert E. Lee—one thing has become increasingly clear: Confederate monuments are not innocent markers of history or heritage. Rather, they reflect the obstinacy of white supremacy in this country. They point to the history of "whiteness" standing its ground against Black progress and equality. They serve as statuary odes to white supremacy cemented into the nation's landscape. This is substantiated not only by the coalition of white supremacists who gathered in Charlottesville and marched with lit torches evocative of Ku Klux Klan rallies and mob lynching but also by the historical relationship between racial progress in America and the erection of these Confederate monuments.

Research conducted by the Southern Poverty Law Center (SPLC) corroborates what historians have long pointed out, that "cities and states—mostly in the South—responded [to racial progress] by erecting such monuments." The research highlights two historical periods in which there were notable spikes in the building of these monuments: "The first began around 1900 as Southern states were enacting Jim Crow laws to disenfranchise African Americans and re-segregate society after several decades of integration that followed Reconstruction. It lasted well into the 1920s, a period that also saw a strong revival of the Ku Klux Klan.... The second period began in the mid-1950s and lasted until the late 1960s, the period encompassing the modern civil rights movement."[3]

Each of these periods reflects a different side of the same coin of white supremacy. On the one hand, the first period has been described as a "nadir" in the struggle for Black equality in the early twentieth century. In many respects, this era was a continued response to the period of Southern Reconstruction, described by W. E. B. Du Bois as a time when "[Black people] went

---

3. "Whose Heritage? Public Symbols of the Confederacy," Southern Poverty Law Center, February 2019, https://www.splcenter.org/20190201/whose-heritage-public-symbols-confederacy.

free; stood a brief moment in the sun; then moved back again toward slavery."[4] This of course was the period during which Woodrow Wilson served two presidential terms. The erecting of monuments, therefore, corresponds with a presidency that indeed attempted to move Black people "back again toward slavery," returning Jim Crow policies to the federal government and *The Birth of a Nation* to the White House. The rise of Confederate monuments during this Black "nadir" reflects "whiteness" on the offense to subjugate and terrorize Black bodies.

On the other hand, the period of 1950s and 1960s is often seen as a "zenith" period in the Black struggle. During this time of civil rights struggle, Black people were fighting to stand again "for a brief moment in the sun." The Supreme Court's 1954 *Brown v. Board of Education* decision opened the door for federal courts to begin striking down Jim Crow laws. The proliferation of Confederate monuments, in this instance, reflected "whiteness" on the defense against such efforts. The increase of Confederate monuments during these two periods epitomizes the "color-line" that Du Bois astutely identified as the problem of the twentieth century. The strategic building of monuments was tantamount to sending Confederate soldiers out to guard that line.

The erection of Confederate memorials initially began following the Civil War, as an effort to provide a "proper burial" for Confederate soldiers whose bones were scattered beneath the ground of farmlands and fields throughout the South. The Ladies Memorial Association (LMA), founded in 1865, led these efforts. These women typically raised money to support the work of finding such remains and preparing cemetery gravesites for their burial. Eventually the LMA organized annual Decoration Days at the gravesites.

---

4. W. E. B. DuBois, *Black Reconstruction in America, 1860–1880*, with an introduction by David Levering Lewis (1935; New York: Free Press, 1992), 30.

As southern whites regained more control of their local and state governments, and as the Reconstruction agenda came to an end with Jim Crow laws and white racist terror organizations, the project of honoring Confederate soldiers began to take on a more overtly white supremacist tone. Historian Jane Censer writes, "By the late 1880s southern efforts to remember had changed from gathering the dead in cemeteries and giving each an individual headstone to glorifying the dead heroes of the Confederacy."[5]

The glorification of Confederate soldiers gained momentum with the 1895 founding of the United Daughters of the Confederacy (UDC). In erecting monuments in public spaces, the UDC turned its attention away from simply honoring the memory of Confederate soldiers to vindicating the Confederacy and its white supremacist cause. As Karen Cox, a leading scholar of UDC history, says, "[The UDC was] part of a campaign to paint the Southern cause in the Civil War as just and slavery as a benevolent institution, and [the monuments'] installation came against a backdrop of Jim Crow violence and oppression of African Americans. The monuments were put up as explicit symbols of white supremacy."[6] Indeed, the UDC became a leading proponent of the "Lost Cause" narrative.

The Lost Cause narrative portrays the Civil War as a battle for "states' rights" rather than for slavery, and it caricatures the enslaved as loyal to their masters and the Confederate cause. But regardless of how fervently the UDC promoted the Lost

---

5. Jane Turner Censer, "Confederate Memorials: Their Past and Future," in *Confederate Statues and Memorialization: History in the Headlines*, edited by Catherine Clinton (Athens: University of Georgia Press, 2019), Kindle edition, 107.

6. Karen L. Cox, "The Whole Point of Confederate Monuments is to Celebrate White Supremacy," *Washington Post*, August 16, 2017, https://www.washingtonpost.com/news/posteverything/wp/2017/08/16/the-whole-point-of-confederate-monuments-is-to-celebrate-white-supremacy/.

Cause version of the Civil War, or how many monuments it put up as a tribute to that war, the narrative was clearly undermined by the declaration issued by the State of South Carolina, which led the way toward secession.

The "Declaration of the Immediate Causes Which Induce and Justify the Secession of South Carolina," issued on December 24, 1860, makes clear that, inasmuch as there was a concern for states' rights, the particular right at issue here was the right of states to maintain slavery. Specifically, the South Carolina declaration points to the U.S. Constitution's Fugitive Slave Clause, Article 4, Section 2, which declares:

> No Person held to Service or Labour in one State, under the Laws thereof, escaping into another, shall, in Consequence of any Law or Regulation therein, be discharged from such Service or Labour, but shall be delivered up of Claim of the Party to whom such Service or Labour may be due.[7]

It is this clause which South Carolina accused the federal government of willfully violating. In the course of making this case, the declaration expressed particular umbrage over the election of President Lincoln. The Declaration reads:

> [I]ncreasing hostility on the part of the non-slaveholding States to the Institution of Slavery has led to a disregard of their obligations, and the laws of the General Government have ceased to effect the objects of the Constitution.... They have denounced as sinful the Institution of Slavery; they have permitted open establishment among them of societies, whose avowed object is to disturb the peace and to eloign the property of the citizens of other States. They have encouraged and assisted thousands of our slaves to leave their homes; and those who remain, have been incited by emissaries, books and

---

7. See https://constitutioncenter.org/interactive-constitution/article/article-iv.

pictures to servile insurrection...and all the States north of that line have united in the election of a man to the high office of President of the United States whose opinions and purposes are hostile to slavery. He is to be entrusted with the administration of the Common Government, because he has declared that that "Government cannot endure permanently half slave, half free," and that the public mind must rest in the belief that slavery is in the course of ultimate extinction.[8]

Again, this Declaration leaves no doubt that slavery was the issue that drove Southern secession. The specific "states' right" for which the Civil War was fought was the right of southern states to make chattel slaves of Black people.

The obvious speciousness of the Lost Cause narrative notwithstanding, the efforts of the UDC to promote this false narrative carried forward. By the end of World War I, Cox reports that the UDC's numbers grew to "an army of 100,000 women, engaged in the fight to preserve and perpetuate the myths that the Confederate cause was a just and honorable one and that states' rights, not slavery, was its call to arms."[9]

In promoting these myths, the UDC was not content with simply erecting stone monuments. It was also determined to create "living monuments" that would perpetuate the Lost Cause narrative, perhaps for generations to come. Thus, the group developed educational materials espousing a Lost Cause version of history to be distributed in schools. It also developed instructional material for "Children of the Confederacy" chapters, which it had established for children six to sixteen years of age. Again, the UDC was determined to indoctrinate a generation of children

---

8. Declaration, https://digital.scetv.org/teachingAmerhistory/pdfs/Dec-ImmCauses.pdf.

9. Karen L. Cox, "The Confederacy's 'Living Monuments,'" *New York Times*, October 6, 2017, https://www.nytimes.com/2017/10/06/opinion/the-confederacys-living-monuments.html?auth=login-email &login=email.

who would "grow up to defend states' rights and white supremacy."[10] To reiterate: these two things went together—the
battle for states' rights was inextricably linked to a crusade for
white supremacy. Lest one imagine that the UDC cause was
anything nobler than that, one simply needs to be reminded of
its support for the Ku Klux Klan. Cox says, "The Daughters regarded the Ku Klux Klan, which had been founded to resist Reconstruction, as a heroic organization, necessary to return order
to the South. Order, of course, meant the use of violence to sub-
due newly freed Blacks."[11]

Cox suggests that the UDC efforts to create "living monuments" were not for naught, as these "Children of the Confederacy" no doubt became the same people who carried Confederate
flags and raged against civil rights activists during the movement of the 1950s and 1960s. Truly, they became living, ranting
monuments to white supremacy.

It was also during the aforementioned two periods in the
twentieth century, which saw an increase in Confederate monuments, that the UDC pursued a campaign to reconcile the South
and the North around their Lost Cause version of history. To this
end, they began to erect monuments and memorials in prominent public spaces in the North also. Their greatest achievement
during this time was arguably the Confederate Memorial installed in Arlington National Cemetery.

The dedication of this monument took place on June 3,
1914, not coincidentally the birthday of Jefferson Davis, the
president of the Confederacy. In its official description, Arlington Cemetery describes the monument as "a nostalgic, mythol-
ogized vision of the Confederacy, including highly sanitized
depictions of slavery." Included in these depictions are "an enslaved woman depicted as a 'Mammy,' holding the infant

10. Cox, "The Confederacy's 'Living Monuments.'"
11. Cox, "Whole Point of Confederate Monuments."

child of a white officer, and an enslaved man following his owner to war." The monument also includes a Latin inscription that directly promotes the Lost Cause ideology: *"Victrix causa diis placuit sed victa Caton"* ("The victorious cause was pleasing to the gods, but the lost cause to Cato")."[12] Significantly, at the time when this monument was dedicated (a culmination of the reinterment of Confederate remains in Arlington Cemetery), Black soldiers were not permitted to be buried in Arlington. In fact, the cemetery remained segregated until 1948, when President Truman issued his order to desegregate the armed forces. Thus, the Confederate monument at Arlington, like similar monuments, served to hold the "color line" of white supremacy.

Another notable success of the UDC's northern campaign during this period was the 1953 installation of stained-glass windows honoring Robert E. Lee and Stonewall Jackson in the Washington National Cathedral. By means of these stained-glass memorials, the UDC bestowed a kind of sacred legitimation on these men as well as on the Lost Cause mythology. In a fitting congruence, the windows were installed in a bay where Woodrow Wilson, the only president to be buried in Washington, DC, had been interred. It was as if these two Confederate generals were standing guard over the remains of one who himself had stood guard over the "color line."

At the same time, running parallel to the resurgence of Confederate monuments was the resurgence of the Confederate flag. In addition to becoming the emblem for "Dixiecrat" politicians in 1948, the Confederate flag became a decided symbol for white supremacy. John Coski, historian and director of the Confederacy Museum in Richmond, notes that, "During the height of the civil rights movement in the 1950s and 1960s, the Confederate

---

12. For description and inscription, see https://www.arlingtoncemetery.mil/Explore/Monuments-and-Memorials/Confederate-Memorial.

battle flag became the opposing symbol to the Stars and Stripes. Identifying themselves with American principles and patriotism, the civil rights protesters marched with the Stars and Stripes. Segregationists played into the protestors' strategy by taunting them with Confederate flags."[13] As was the case with the Confederate monuments, the flag reflected white resistance to Black equality. At the time, the *Chicago Defender*, a leading Black newspaper, aptly noted: "In a large measure the rebel craze is an ugly reaction to the remarkable progress of our group."[14]

What this brief history makes unmistakably clear is that the placement of Confederate monuments on the public square has never been innocent. Rather, it has been pernicious. As even the great-great grandsons of Stonewall Jackson recognized, "Confederate monuments like the Jackson statue were never intended as benign symbols. Rather, they were the clearly articulated artwork of white supremacy."[15]

White supremacists erected Confederate monuments not only to control how the past was to be remembered but also to control how the present was to be conceived. This is why Confederate monuments reflect more than just the privilege to control public space. More insidiously, they exemplify social-cultural epistemological privilege. This is the privilege to control public knowing.

---

13. John M. Coski, *The Confederate Battle Flag: America's Most Embattled Emblem* (Cambridge, MA: The Belknap Press of Harvard University Press, 2005), Kindle edition location, 1701.

14. Quoted in Yoni Appelbaum, "Why Is the Flag Still There?" *The Atlantic*, June 20, 2015, https://www.theatlantic.com/politics/archive/2015/06/why-is-the-flag-still-there/396431/.

15. Jack Christian and Warren Christian, "The Monuments Must Go: An Open Letter from the Great-Great-Grandsons of Stonewall Jackson," *Slate*, August 16, 2017, slate.com/news-and-politics/2017/08/stonewall-jacksons-grandsons-the-monuments-must-go.html.

Social-Cultural Epistemological Privilege

Social-cultural epistemological privilege is about the knowledge that the social collective receives from the public square. This knowledge suggests the normative story through which to judge and evaluate information regarding "shared history" and even shared experiences. The normative story sets the standard for whose knowledge is acceptable for interpreting and evaluating reality. Social-cultural epistemological privilege effectively reifies a gaze through which all public knowledge, be it knowledge of the past or of the present, is to be considered. It is the gaze of the dominant social-cultural group. In this instance, it is the gaze of whiteness.

While a white gaze is the inevitable result of a country founded on the premise of white supremacy, the persistence of this gaze reinforces its ideological foundation. There is an intrinsic circularity, in that the white gaze is produced by a white supremacist foundation even as it functions to sustain the notion of white supremacy. Any "disconfirming" information, when it comes to the preeminence of whiteness, "is filtered out or marginalized."[16] This is the way social-cultural epistemological privilege functions. Philosopher Charles Mills might describe it as part of a white "non-knowing" wherein the "white delusion of racial superiority insulates itself against refutation."[17] In the end, this epistemological privilege works to ensure that a white supremacist agenda will continue to be enacted across generations.

This social-cultural epistemological privilege does not function in an ideological vacuum. It interacts with and reinforces the anti-Black narrative. To reiterate, the anti-Black narrative

---

16. Charles W. Mills, *Black Rights/White Wrongs: The Critique of Racial Liberalism* (New York: Oxford University Press, 2017), 61.

17. Mills, *Black Rights/White Wrongs*, 55. This discussion is formed by Charles Mills's discussion of non-knowing and the social epistemology.

cast Black people as dangerous beasts ruled by uncontrollable passion, not reason. The "epistemological" consequence is that Black "knowing," even if it is an interpretation of a Black experience, is "discredited in advance as being epistemologically suspect." The point of the matter is that the interface of the anti-Black narrative with white epistemological privilege literally renders the notion of Black knowing an oxymoron. Black people have no social-cultural epistemic authority. As we will later see, this is consequential for Black bodies in the public square.

In general, the social-cultural epistemological privilege of whiteness has far-reaching implications for the nation's social and cultural realities. Perhaps most significant are its implications for the nation's moral imaginary. In setting the norm of authoritative knowing, the social-cultural epistemological privilege of whiteness influences judgments concerning justice and injustice. Its influence on the moral imaginary will become clearer as we examine the role of Confederate monuments in furthering the social-cultural epistemological privilege of whiteness.

Confederate monuments are significant arbiters of this privilege. They also function as conceptual symbols and symbols of social memory. When we understand this, we can more fully appreciate why their presence on the public square has become such a contested issue and a focal point of protest during this time of racial reckoning.

Confederate Monuments as Conceptual Symbols

Paul Tillich, an esteemed theologian of culture, reminds us that two of the characteristic features of symbols is that they "point beyond themselves to something else" and that they "participate in what they point to."[18] As conceptual symbols, Confederate monuments do indeed have meaning beyond their physical

---

18. Paul Tillich, *Dynamics of Faith* (New York: Harper and Brothers, 1957), 47–48.

presence. They "point beyond themselves" to a particular conception of reality. They symbolize a white conceptual frame for understanding the natural order of the world. Borrowing from the words of Peter Berger, as conceptual symbols, the Confederate monuments "are endowed with an ontological status" that suggests the "universal order of things and, consequently, one's own being in this order."[19] That is, inasmuch as Confederate monuments reflect a white supremacist ordering of society, they project this order into universal reality. In Berger's words, a human-constructed "nomos" is projected into the "cosmos," so that the white supremacist society serves as a "microcosmic reflection . . . of the universe as such." Consequently, the privileged conceptual vantage point for comprehending the cosmos is a "white" vantage point.

It is in this way that the monuments represent more than the men they depict. Rather, they signify a way of conceiving the world and locating one's place within it. In so doing, these monuments participate in what they point to. As the very statues themselves epitomize a white supremacist order of reality, they virtually become extensions of that reality. At the very least, they represent a key to comprehending the nature of reality. The knowledge value they provide transcends the facts of the "Civil War." That is why it does not matter if the Lost Cause narrative they project is factually correct or not. The knowledge value of the Lost Cause narrative is its affirmation of a white supremacist conceptual framework for adjudicating knowledge about the world itself.

As conceptual symbols, Confederate monuments serve to "orient" people toward a way of knowing the world. They project whiteness into the wider epistemological cosmos as the normative vantage point for engaging and interpreting reality. The ethnocentric perspective of whiteness becomes the key to understanding and unlocking knowledge about the cosmos itself.

---

19. Peter Berger, *The Sacred Canopy: Elements of a Sociological Theory of Religion* (New York: Anchor Books, 1967), 24.

It is in this way that the social-cultural privilege of whiteness becomes more than simply a social construction. It is the privileged way of knowing because it reflects the transcendent order. Confederate monuments as conceptual symbols help anchor white epistemological privilege in transcendent reality, making that privilege appear co-extensive with the cosmos. As we shall see, this is one of the reasons so much furor is raised around efforts to remove these monuments from the public square.

In the end, those raced white are able to see the world and themselves "*through* the [conceptual symbol] itself."[20] Inasmuch, therefore, as these monuments suggest something about the world and reality, they also say something about the people who create and sustain them. Their very whiteness takes on "cosmic" proportions; they virtually see themselves as the center of the universe. White supremacy, therefore, is masked as it becomes the order of things. This becomes even clearer as we delve deeper into understanding the way in which Confederate monuments act as symbols of social memory. Before looking at that, however, I want to say a word about the UDC's stained-glass "monuments" to Lee and Jackson in the Washington National Cathedral.

Ironically, I had been working at the Cathedral for at least a year before I knew that the Lee/Jackson windows were even there, and that was only when the dean of the Cathedral, Gary Hall, called for their removal following the white-supremacist-motivated massacre of nine Black people at Emanuel A.M.E. Church in Charleston, South Carolina, in 2015. Needless to say, it was a surprise, if not theologically disorienting, to realize that Confederate windows had found a comfortable home in the Washington National Cathedral for almost forty years. It was not lost on me that the placement of Confederate memorials or icons within sacred space carried an additional meaning

---

20. Mills, *Black Rights/White Wrongs*, 63.

beyond that of their display on the public square: in effect, they became sacred symbols, bearing religious and theological implications.

Historically, the use of stained-glass windows within religious spaces was not simply for aesthetic purposes. They were typically used as an educational or catechetical tool to teach certain spiritual and religious values. Within medieval churches, for instance, they were used as a way of teaching biblical stories to those who were illiterate or could not afford Bibles. Beyond biblical history, these windows were also vehicles for imparting church history, or representing the saints of the church. In general, the central purpose of stained-glass windows within religious spaces was to inspire the "faithful" through the stories and figures they represent.

The intent of the Washington National Cathedral's Lee-Jackson windows seemed to follow this pattern. As Civil War historian Chris Mackowski says, by being memorialized in the National Cathedral, Lee and Jackson found a place where "Gods and Generals" live. And, thus, within the Cathedral they stand "side by side" as "Christian soldiers."[21]

In fact, the inscriptions below the windows leave no doubt concerning the story these windows were meant to tell. Below the Lee window, he is described as a "servant of God, leader of men, general-in-chief of the armies of the Confederate States whose compelling sense of duty, serene faith, and unfailing courtesy mark him for all ages as a Christian solider."[22]

---

21. Chris Mackowski, "Lee and Jackson in the National Cathedral," *Emerging Civil War*, March 22, 2012, https://emergingcivilwar.com/2012/03/22/lee-and-jackson-in-the-national-cathedral/.

22. While these inscriptions are included in the Mackowski article, my reporting here comes from my own viewing of the windows. As a member of the task force to have them removed, I viewed and studied them numerous times. See, for instance, Heather Beasley Doyle, "National Cathedral Continues to Debate the Lee, Jackson Windows," Episcopal News Service, February 20, 2017, https://www.episcopalnewsservice.org/2017/02/20/

The inscription beneath the Jackson window describes him as one who "walked humbly before his Creator." Of course, nowhere in the windows—which depict the two men in different stages of their lives—is there any hint of slavery, the cause for which they fought. Instead, they are depicted as men on a Christian journey, exemplars to others on a religious/spiritual journey. And thus, the mission of the UDC itself was cast in a spiritual light. That seems to have been the UDC's intention, as reflected in the words of the memorial's project director in a final report in 1953:

> These memorials … in this great temple of worship, dedicated to the glory of God and the good of Mankind, are memorials not only to Robert E. Lee and to "Stonewall" Jackson, to the Confederate Government and the principles for which it stood, but in the years to come, a Memorial to the United Daughters of the Confederacy in America's Westminster Abbey among the nation's Great and Good, and will attest to the world our interest in things spiritual and that we passed this Way, the Way of Truth and Light.[23]

In addition to telling a story of two men on a Christian journey, the memorialization of Lee and Jackson in a sacred space has the effect of casting them as theological symbols. As such, the Lee-Jackson windows indicate not only something about the people and culture that gave birth to them, but also something about God. Further, a display of these men within sacred spaces insinuates theological legitimacy for white supremacist ideologies and values. Such a display provides a sacred canopy over

---

national-cathedral-continues-to-debate-the-lee-jackson-windows/; https://www.washingtonpost.com/local/washington-national-cathedral-is-taking-its-time-to-ponder-its-confederate-windows/2017/06/28/f85c6ece-5c05-11e7-9fc6-c7ef4bc58d13_story.html.

23. Quoted in Mackowski, "Lee and Jackson in National Cathedral."

the Lost Cause narrative, which of course was the intention of the UDC in placing these memorials there. The UDC reportedly represented the memorials to prospective donors in the following way:

> Here, where the nation's heroes are to be honored side by side, the patriotism of the Confederacy shall have recognition. No boy from either side of the line must ever stand in this great gathering of soldiers and wonder at the absence of a Southern hero. One must be there lest the question be: were the men who wore the Gray really patriots; did they fight for their country to keep it the way their forebears founded it? They were and they did; and, for their sake, their beloved leader must have a place where the great spirits of our nation's history are to be enshrined.[24]

In the final analysis, just as the monuments, as conceptual symbols, project a white way of knowing onto the cosmos, as sacred symbols they project whiteness onto God. As Tillich says, "Religious symbols point symbolically to that which transcends them"—in this instance, God. It is as if God blesses the Confederacy and its values. Hence, as religious symbols the stained-glass monuments to Lee and Jackson imply that God is a white supremacist, and therefore that not all persons are equal in God's sight. Put in those terms, it should be obvious that the placement of Confederate symbols in sacred spaces is a kind of blasphemy, a denial of a just and loving God for whom there is "neither slave nor free." More on this will follow in Part 2 of this book. But for now, it is important to recognize how Confederate monuments as religions and theological symbols serve to reinforce the social-cultural epistemological privilege of whiteness by covering it with a "sacred canopy," thereby granting it divine affirmation.

---

24. Mackowski, "Lee and Jackson in National Cathedral."

Confederate Monuments: Symbols of Social Memory

Symbols of social memory, like conceptual symbols, "help us make sense of the world we live in."[25] Overall, as we will soon see, social memory is the "discursive" power of social-cultural epistemological privilege in the public square. Social memory is a constructed memory. The historically dominant social group shapes social memory. It is a memory constructed to sustain a narrative that supports the perspective and agenda of the social-cultural dominant group. In this sense, social memory exposes relationships of power, even as it sustains "social boundaries...and power."[26] It does this, historian John Gillis points out, by determining what is important to "be remembered (or forgotten)."[27] It is through social memory, therefore, that a particular story is made normative while another is marginalized, if not actually erased. First of all, then, social memory becomes the framework through which a nation's history is to be read. In other words, social memory helps to construct and promote the "official" story of a nation. It provides the knowledge base that defines social-cultural epistemological privilege.

Next, as social memory creates an official history, it also forges an official identity. The two are inextricably related. The nation's official history (the story of those whose history defines the nation) shapes the national identity, while at the same time the national identity shapes the remembered history. As Gillis explains, "the notion of identity depends on the idea of memory, and vice versa."[28] He goes on to say that "a sense of sameness [i.e., national

---

25. John R. Gillis, "Memory and Identity: The History of a Relationship," in *Commemorations: The Politics of National Identity*, edited by John R. Gillis (Princeton, NJ: Princeton University Press, 1994), 3.

26. Gillis, "Memory and Identity," 3.

27. Gillis, "Memory and Identity," 3.

28. Gillis, "Memory and Identity," 3.

identity] over time and space is sustained by remembering; and what is remembered is defined by the assumed identity."[29]

To recapitulate, social memory creates an "official" story/ history, thus establishing a normative national identity. In so doing, it clarifies what history matters, what is remembered, and how it is to be remembered or interpreted. For a country built on a white supremacist foundation, social memory serves to preserve that founding identity. The "white" story, therefore, is elevated as the normative story. Any story that challenges the white normative story is viewed not just as a contesting narrative, but as a false one. Charles Mills provides an apt summary of how social memory functions in this manner. He says:

> There will be both official and counter-memory, with conflicting judgments about what is important in the past and what is unimportant, what happened and what does matter, what happened and does not matter, and what did not happen at all. So applying this to race, we will find an intimate relationship between white identity, white memory, white amnesia.[30]

Finally, then, for a country built on a white supremacist foundation, the over-riding function of social memory is to promote and preserve white hegemonic power. By reading the nation's history through a white lens and thus elevating the white story as the normative "official" story, white supremacy appears to be an organic and inevitable outcome of history. It is here that Michel Foucault's insight into how hegemonic power is most effectively sustained becomes helpful in understanding the significance of social memory as the discursive power of social-cultural epistemological privilege.

Foucault stresses that power is most effective not by being aggressively coercive or repressive, but by being productive and

---

29. Gillis, "Memory and Identity," 3.

30. Mills, *Black Rights/White Wrongs*, 65.

discursive. Power produces the knowledge it needs to legitimate itself, a process Foucault calls the "will to knowledge." In this regard, social memory is a part of that process. In serving as the hermeneutic frame through which history is remembered, social memory represents that "will" to knowledge. As the content derived from a particular interpretative engagement with history, it is the knowledge itself. This knowledge, that is social memory, is then carefully deployed through discourse. "Discourse," Foucault says, "transmits and produces power; it reinforces it."[31] Essentially, as we have shown, the discourse that is social memory produces and reinforces white supremacist power.

Now how precisely is this discourse deployed? It is deployed through social institutions such as educational and religious institutions, or through material and non-material artifacts in the public square. It is through these artifacts, as Mills might say, that power is "generated and regenerated in ceremonies and official holidays, concretized in statues, parks and monuments."[32]

It is important to remember that, as we have seen in recounting the history of Confederate public statuary, monuments are not incidental parts of the national landscape, erected to simply enhance or add beauty to the public square. Neither do they arise, as historian Kirk Savage notes, "as if by natural law to celebrate the deserving." Rather, "they are built by people with sufficient power to marshal or impose" their remembering of history onto the public square, and thereby onto others.[33] As Savage explains, "Monuments served to anchor collective remembering.... Monuments embodied and legitimated the very notion of a common memory and by extension the notion of a people who possessed and rallied

---

31. Michel Foucault, *The History of Sexuality: Volume 1: An Introduction*, translated by Robert Hurley (New York: Vintage Books, 1990), 101.

32. Mills, *Black Rights/White Wrongs*, 64.

33. Kirk Savage, "The Politics of Memory: Black Emancipation and the Civil War Monument," in Gillis, *Commemorations*, 135.

around such a memory."[34] It is interesting to recognize within Savage's explication of the significance of monuments the crucial relationship he alludes to between a people's remembering and a people's identity. In the end, monuments are literally social memory "made marble and concrete."[35] They "work to impose a permanent memory on the very landscape within which we order our lives."[36] This brings us to the significance of Confederate monuments as symbols of social memory.

Confederate monuments are symbols of social memory as they point beyond themselves. But in this instance, they point not to a conceptual understanding of the world but to the American story and identity. Thus, it does not matter that Confederate leaders are presented as patriots, and not as traitors; as fighting to preserve states' rights, and not to preserve slavery. Once again, the significance of Confederate monuments is not because of the particular tale they tell, but because in this case they represent a particular interpretation of the nation's history and identity. Symbolized in Confederate monuments, in other words, is an official history and identity.

What cannot be emphasized enough is that these monuments, in forging a social memory that reinforces the nation's story and identity, do so in a way that mystifies—if not negates—the fact of white supremacy. They allow the American story to be understood in a way that covers up the intentional fostering of systemic, structural, and ideological white racism. As Confederate monuments conceal "the true history of the Confederate States of America and the seven decades of Jim Crow segregation and oppression that followed the Reconstruction era," they likewise conceal the true reality of white supremacy.[37] They make

---

34. Savage, "The Politics of Memory," 130–31.

35. Mills, *Black Rights/White Wrongs*, 66.

36. Savage, "The Politics of Memory," 143.

37. "Whose Heritage? Public Symbols of the Confederacy."

white dominance appear to be a natural fact of history, not a consequence of the intentional implementation of white racist injustice. Only white people—not Black people, Native Americans, or any other people not raced white—appear as active agents in the American story. Thus, white people are depicted at the center of the nation's history because that is what they are.

Subtly fostered though this social memory is the Anglo-Saxon myth of white people as naturally more motivated, industrious, and intelligent than other races of people. And again, social memory presents this not as a consequence of white supremacist intentionality but rather as a fact of history. What is a subjective rendering of history becomes an objective fact in social memory. Essentially, social memory works to mask "the long history of structural discrimination that has left whites with the differential resources they have today and all its consequent advantages in negotiating opportunity structures."[38] This is how discursive power works. As Confederate monuments find prominence in public spaces, they at once both mystify and "unlock" this white supremacist story and identity, deploying it on the public square.

This brings us to another aspect of symbols. As Tillich says, they "open up hidden depths of our own being" that "correspond to the elements of reality that they point to." For those who define themselves in relationship to uninterrogated "whiteness," the Confederate monuments, as symbols of social memory, open up hidden depths of their own being and connect them to a profound sense of self—the deeper meaning of who they are.

This is particularly important for those raced white who, despite their whiteness, are marginalized in society because of some economic, educational, or other factor of societal status. The monuments endow them with a sense of importance. As they identify with the "white story," and inasmuch as the white

---

38. Mills, *Black Rights/White Wrongs*, 63.

story is presented as the defining center of the American story, they are brought from the powerless edges of society to the powerful center. Borrowing from the words of Erich Fromm, "The meaning of their life and the identity of self are determined" by the very story that these monuments promulgate.[39] Thus, what Savage says about local communities earning "credibility by their assimilation into a national memory" applies to the white disenfranchised.[40] They earn status and credibility by their assimilation into a national memory/identity. Put another way, a disempowered "white" collective is empowered by the very power that is displayed through the soldiers depicted in the monuments. Savage puts it this way with regard to the White and Anglo-Saxon: "They offer up not a neutral body, but a collective body with certain boundaries and privileges." Figuratively, if not literally, those in the white collective see themselves in the very powerful bodies of the Confederate soldiers. Therefore, these Confederate monuments "unlock" the power of white identity, which for some may otherwise have been hidden and thus seemingly unattainable.

At this point it is also important to remember, as noted in chapter 1, that whiteness as a racial construct finds its meaning only in dominating opposition to those not raced white. For those persons who have consciously embraced what it means to be raced white, their very sense of self is grounded in oppositional relationships of power and superiority. Put simply, their meaning is found in the ability to show dominance over those otherwise raced. Since Blackness is constructed as the polar opposite of whiteness, there is no greater display of white dominance than when it is acting itself out in relationship to Black bodies. Understanding this helps explain why Confederate

---

39. Erich Fromm, *Escape from Freedom* (New York/Toronto: Rinehart and Company, Inc., 1941), 156.

40. Savage, "Politics of Memory," 131.

monuments have historically proliferated on the public square in the context of defiance of Black progress. This pattern further establishes the symbolic nature of these monuments. For again, the timing of their erection points to their relevance beyond their status as artifacts of history. This timing is a symbolic display of authoritarian dominance, an assertion of the rightness of a white conception of reality as well as a rendering of the (official) national story and identity.

We come then to the violence that sometimes erupts in attempts to remove Confederate monuments from the public square (as happened in the aforementioned Charlottesville incident). To repeat, whiteness is an oppositional identity construct that characteristically degrades the humanity of others. As such, it is violent. Anything that denies or belittles another's humanity is violent. To remove the monuments from the public square creates a profound disorientation. It not only disrupts a people's conceptual framework—which again is about how they see the world—but it also attacks their identity. Removing these monuments therefore invalidates a way of both knowing the world and of seeing oneself. It is virtually an act that disavows the salience of "white" identity. And so, the violence that is unleashed when these monuments are threatened is the "hidden" violence that is endemic to white identity itself. Such overt violence is almost inevitable. Once again we are reminded of Tillich's observation that symbols "unlock dimensions and elements of our [being] which correspond to the dimensions and elements of reality." Whiteness *is* a violent construct. A white conception of reality is likewise violent. Hence, as symbols, Confederate monuments encapsulate the inherent violence of the whiteness they represent, and this implicit violence is unlocked and released whenever these symbols are threatened.

Now, before assessing the overall significance of these monuments for white social-cultural epistemological privilege and the subsequent implications for the moral imaginary, it is important to recognize that Confederate monuments are not the only monuments on the public landscape. They do not carry the sole burden of social memory. Together with them, various other monuments forge the national story and identity as a white story. Nevertheless, Confederate monuments do play a unique role when it comes to social memory. This uniqueness is made evident by their disproportionate presence on the public square.

The SPLC reports, for instance, that there are about 1,500 symbols of the Confederacy in public spaces, about 718 of which are monuments.[41] As researcher Shelley Puhak observes, "The number of U.S. monuments honoring the Confederacy eclipse those U.S. monuments honoring any other cause or group of people in American history."[42] She goes on to say, "there are *seven times* as many statues honoring the Confederacy as there are statues lauding America's Founding Fathers.... [Confederate monuments] can be found in at least thirty-one states, including in states like Montana."[43] A further indication of the significance of these monuments in defining the nation's story and identity is that at least thirty-four have been added to the public landscape since 2000.

Just as telling of the significance for social memory of such monuments on the public square is the message conveyed by those that are not there. Given the focus on the Civil War era, notably missing is a significant presence of monuments to the Black struggle to be free from the bonds of chattel slavery, let alone monuments that even acknowledge slavery itself. Mayor Mitch Landrieu, in his speech regarding the removal of Confederate monuments in New Orleans, gave powerful testimony to this fact. He said,

---

41. "Whose Heritage? Public Symbols of the Confederacy."

42. Shelley Puhak, "Confederate Monuments and Tributes in the United States Explained," in Catherine Clinton et al., *Confederate Statues and Memorialization* (Athens: University of Georgia Press, 2019), 86.

43. Puhak, "Confederate Monuments," 86.

So when people say to me that the monuments in question are history, well,…it immediately begs the question why there are no slave ship monuments? No prominent markers on public land to remember the lynchings or the slave blocks? Nothing to remember this long chapter of our lives of pain, of sacrifice, of shame…? So for those self-appointed defenders of history and the monuments, they are eerily silent on what amounts to historical malfeasance, a lie by omission.[44]

Even in the monuments reflecting the Union story, the Black presence is notably absent. And, when Black people are included in the monuments depicting that period, they are typically portrayed as a subordinate part of the white narrative, if not as supplicants. One of the most controversial presentations in this regard is the Thomas Ball Emancipation Monument dedicated in 1867. This monument honors Abraham Lincoln as the "Great Emancipator." In so doing, it portrays a Black person kneeling before Lincoln, as if paying homage to the "great white liberator" for freeing him. In the words of Savage, it shows a "servile figure of the slave receiving the savior's blessing."[45] This portrayal aligns with the wider story of social memory that presents white people as *the* active agents in history, even in the fight against slavery. In general, with regard to recognizing Black leadership in the Black struggle for freedom, Puhak observes, "When added together, the total number of statues honoring two great civil rights leaders, Frederick Douglass and Dr. Martin Luther King Jr.—who each boast seven…[these] are still less than the nearly twenty statues erected to glorify Jefferson Davis, president of the Confederacy.[46] Numbers like these serve

---

44. Mayor Mitch Landrieu Speech Transcript on Removal of Confederate Monuments, May 23, 2017, https://www.rev.com/blog/transcripts/mayor-mitch-landrieu-speech-on-removal-of-confederate-monuments.

45. Savage, "Politics of Memory," 140. See Savage as well for an in-depth discussion of other Civil War monuments with Black representation.

to remind us that social memory is constituted as much by what is erased as by what is remembered from the nation's history. In the words of Mayor Landrieu, "One story told, one story forgotten or maybe even purposefully ignored."[47] By erasing the Black story from social memory, white supremacy is protected, while the sense of Black submissiveness is maintained.

Overall, what we see is the way in which Confederate monuments, with their outsized presence on the public square, have in fact become the prevailing symbols of social memory. In one sense, that they are so prominent is revealing of what was really at stake during the Civil War. Inasmuch as slavery was the central defining issue over which the war was fought, it was a conflict between the nation's white supremacist foundation and its soul. The question was whether or not this nation was going to be a slave nation, hence a white nation, or indeed a nation that recognized the "inalienable rights of all peoples." His own ambivalence regarding the equality of Black people notwithstanding, this is why in his first inaugural address, Lincoln implored the nation to be "touched by its better angels" and to find a way to resolve the problem of slavery. Lincoln recognized that the nation's very soul was at stake. With the defeat of the slaveholding states, the nation's soul-driven vision triumphed, at least for the time being. In the words of Du Bois, it stood in the sun of the nation's democracy, at least for the moment. What historian Eric Foner describes as a "second founding" was actually a second chance for the nation to be guided by the urgings of its soul, which was able to break through in the Declaration of Independence. But, of course, as fleeting as the vision was in the Declaration, it was just as fleeting after the Civil War, as Reconstruction came to a definitive end with the 1877 compromise that put Rutherford B. Hayes into the White House.

---

46. Puhak, "Confederate Monuments," 87.

47. Landrieu, Speech on Removal of Confederate Monuments.

To understand the nation's story through the lens of an ideological/theological struggle is to realize that the Confederate monuments do indeed reflect a signature period in the nation's history. The fact that they find such a prominent place on the public square signifies the nation's ongoing war between its "whiteness" and its soul. They in fact speak to a defining truth about a nation at war with itself.

Overall, as symbols of social memory and conceptual symbols, the Confederate monuments reify the social-cultural epistemological privilege that is whiteness. They are the persistent reminders of that privilege in the public square. As symbols they help to insinuate the sense of white privilege into the collective epistemological consciousness of the public, in a way that is almost immutable. They render anything other than a "white" way of knowing unreasonable and fraudulent. Essentially, they make it virtually impossible for society to tolerate a "truth" that is not white—be it historical or otherwise. Hence, social-cultural epistemological privilege is not benign. It is not an abstract notional matter. It has practical consequences for peoples' lived realities. For non-white people, especially Black people, those consequences can be life-changing and fatal. So, let us now turn to the way in which the social-cultural privilege of whiteness plays itself out in the public square before looking at its implications for the nation's moral imagery and the future of these monuments in the public square.

The Implications of White Knowing

On September 17, 2020, President Trump held a hastily arranged White House Conference on American History. As if to lend it greater credibility, the conference was held in the rotunda of the National Archives—even though the Archives did not sponsor or have a role in organizing it. During the event, Trump announced the creation of the 1776 Commission "to promote patriotic education." He believed there was an urgent need for this commission to confront what he alleged was a movement that "warped, distorted, and defiled the American story with deceptions, falsehoods, and lies." Of this danger, there was "no better example," he said, than the "1619 Project."

The 1619 Project was a Pulitzer Prize-winning *New York Times* essay series led by award-winning investigative journalist Nikole Hannah-Jones. In a letter that served as a preface to the essays, Jake Silverstein, editor-in-chief of the *New York Times Magazine*, said: "The goal of The 1619 Project is to reframe American history by considering what it would mean to regard 1619 [the year when enslaved Africans first landed in Virginia] as our nation's birth year. Doing so," Silverstein continued, "requires us to place the consequences of slavery and the contributions of black Americans at the very center of the story we tell ourselves about who we are as a country."[48]

What followed was a series of essays from a range of scholars with expertise in diverse fields of study. These essays argued: "Out of slavery—and the anti-Black racism it required—grew nearly everything that has truly made America exceptional...from 'economic might'" to 'endemic racial fears.'"[49] The essay project ultimately attested that Black people have been instrumental in keeping America's democratic vision alive. Nikole Hannah-Jones put it this way: "Our founding ideals of liberty and equality were false when they were written. Black Americans fought to make them true. Without this struggle, America would have no democracy at all."[50]

---

48. Jake Silverstein, The 1619 Project, *New York Times Magazine*, August 18, 2019, 4, https://www.nytimes.com/interactive/2019/08/14/magazine/black-history-american-democracy.html.

49. Silverstein, The 1619 Project, 4.

50. Nikole Hannah-Jones, "The Idea of America," The 1619 Project, *New York Times Magazine*, August 18, 2019, 14, https://www.nytimes.com/interactive/2019/08/14/magazine/black-history-american-democracy. html.

In fewer than a hundred pages, The Project dared to challenge the social memory that fuels the social-cultural epistemological privilege of whiteness. Further, it did so by placing
Blackness at the center of the nation's story. But because whiteness cannot share physical space in the public arena, because it
cannot share epistemological space, it fell inevitably to the architect of the "Make America Great Again" vision to invalidate the
project and the story it told. In doing this, President Trump perfectly exemplified the very way in which white epistemological
privilege works. Like the identity it serves to protect, this privilege is subjugating and oppositional; it cannot accommodate
anything that would challenge an assessment of the American
story as anything less than a white story.

White epistemological privilege regards any form of Black
knowing as abhorrent. Thus, it stands its ground by discrediting
the knowledge of those not raced white, and virtually casts Black
stories as treasonous and "un-American." In the words of Trump,
The 1619 Project and other efforts like it, bore "a striking resem-
blance to the anti-American propaganda of our adversaries."
Moreover, evincing the symbolic significance of Confederate
monuments in fostering the social-cultural epistemological privilege of whiteness, Trump linked The 1619 Project to the efforts to
remove these monuments. He opened the Conference by warning
that "a radical movement is attempting to demolish this treasured
and precious inheritance. [They] have torn down statues of our
founders, desecrated our memorials." These comments echoed a
tweet cited earlier in which Trump lamented, "Sad to see the history and culture of our great country being ripped apart with the
removal of our beautiful statues and monuments."

Trump was not alone in alleging that The 1619 Project was
an unpatriotic rendering of the nation's story. Prior to the White
House Conference, Arkansas senator Tom Cotton (R., Ark.) in-
troduced a bill, the "Saving American History Act of 2020," to
prevent the use of federal funds to teach The 1619 Project in
public schools. In announcing the bill he said, "The *New York*

Times's 1619 Project is a racially divisive, revisionist account of history that denies the noble principles of freedom and equality on which our nation was founded. Not a single cent of federal funding should go to indoctrinate young Americans with this left-wing garbage."

Ironically, while The 1619 Project was proclaimed to be all but "treasonous" propaganda that should not be taught in public schools, there were at least 103 public schools and three colleges named for the Confederate leaders who were actually seditious, including several named for Nathan Bedford Forrest, the Confederate soldier who was also the first grand wizard of the Ku Klux Klan. Clearly then, what most concerned Trump and Cotton was not treasonous disloyalty to the nation. It was disloyalty to a white way of knowing, disloyalty to white supremacist rule. As for the naming of educational institutions for defenders of white supremacy, that only further reveals the insidious reality of discursive power. Not only does it validate what these white supremacists stood for, but it also serves as a brazen assertion of white social-cultural epistemological privilege. It makes clear the standard and frame through which all knowledge is to be assessed.

The responses of Trump and Cotton to The 1619 Project are part of a long historical pattern of the way white epistemological privilege interacts with an anti-Black narrative to invalidate Black people's ability to know, even when it comes to their own experiences. Their responses are, in fact, eerily similar to the reactions by white scholars to narratives of enslaved persons following the Civil War. During that time, "those few scholars who knew the narratives disclaimed them as misleading, inaccurate, tainted."[51] If the enslaved narratives were to be regarded as legitimate, they often required validation from at least one notable

---

51. John Sekora, "Black Message/White Envelope: Genre, Authenticity, and Authority in the Antebellum Slave Narrative," *Callaloo* 32 (1987): 482–515, JSTOR, www.jstor.org/stable/2930465.

white person. It is for this reason that Harriet Jacobs's narrative, *Incidents in the Life of a Slave Girl*, is preceded by a letter from Lydia Maria Child. Child attests that "The author of the following autobiography is known to her." Even what has become a classic narrative, authored by a respected statesman in his own day, needed the validation of two white abolitionists. Frederick Douglass's narrative of his escape from slavery to freedom is preceded by a preface from William Lloyd Garrison along with a letter from Wendell Phillips, authenticating Douglass's experience. Likewise, Phillis Wheatley's *Poems on Various Subjects, Religious and Moral, Negro Servant to Mr. John Wheatley of Boston* is prefaced by "attestation from the most respectable Characters in Boston..." to "assure the World, that the POEMS specified in the following Page were...written by Phillis, a young Negro Girl, who was but a few Years since, brought an uncultivated Barbarian from Africa." It went on to say, "She has been examined by some of the best Judges, and is thought qualified to write them."

What we see, overall, is that in repudiating The 1619 Project, Trump and Cotton shamelessly exemplified a legacy of slavery that is often ignored: the congenial and easy relationship between the anti-Black narrative and white social-cultural epistemological privilege. To reiterate, as these two ideologies interface, Black knowing is wholly invalidated unless it receives white authentication. In the end, the notion that Black people are virtually bereft of reason is reinforced by white social-cultural epistemological privilege. What is made clear is that the interface between white epistemological privilege and an anti-Black narrative is inevitable; they function as different sides of the same coin of white supremacy.

Furthermore, what becomes abundantly clear is that the impact of this privilege is not just academic. While its influence on curricula and the discourse that is deployed in schools is certainly not benign (as we saw in terms of the UDC's educational efforts), white social-cultural epistemology manifests itself in the public square in a more directly dangerous way. It literally imperils Black lives. As we saw in the previous chapter, an anti-Black narrative can trigger instinctive responses to the Black body, resulting in volatile encounters. At the same time, white social-cultural epistemological privilege summarily pre-empts the acceptance of Black people's testimony of these encounters. Mills refers to this as "epistemic presumption against [Black] credibility."[52]

I will never forget an incident that took place during my son's middle school years. A white female student accused him of verbally abusing her with language I had never heard my son use and doubted he knew. The white female director of the school immediately believed my son's accuser, despite the fact that my son had never been in trouble at the school, whereas the girl had. Not even the testimony of two Black teachers, who witnessed part of the interaction, could convince the director that the girl's accusation was false. I was called by one of the Black teachers to come to the school immediately because my son was about to be unjustly suspended. It was not until the girl's mother, though she was not a witness to the event, said that she believed my son was being truthful did the director rescind the suspension—though without an apology to my son or consequences for the girl who had falsely accused him.

This incident was troubling on several levels. At the very least, it showed that a white child's testimony held more credence than even that of two Black adults. Even more disturbing was the fact that already implanted within the white girl's consciousness was a sense of her white epistemological privilege. She knew that she could falsely accuse a Black person and get away with it. Only another white person could invalidate her story.

This incident was not unusual. I have commiserated with other Black parents concerning similar incidents with their children. Moreover, what my son and the Black teachers experienced

---

52. Mills, *Black Rights/White Wrongs*, 68.

in the classroom has a historical counterpart in the courtroom. There is a longstanding pattern of Black testimony being invalidated, especially if it is counter to white testimony. As historian Leon Litwack points out, even if emancipation provided Black people with the opportunity to testify in court, notwithstanding white intimidation of Black witnesses, the refusal of courts "to grant Black testimony credibility" nullified that opportunity.[53] Studies have shown that the perception of Black witnesses as being less credible continues to plague the legal and judicial system today, even in the case of judges.[54] Again, it cannot be emphasized enough that white epistemological privilege in combination with an anti-Black narrative has real consequences. This is made ever clearer as we see the interplay of these two narratives in the daily lives of Black people.

To reiterate, white people continue to call the police on Black people for going about their own business because they know that they will be believed. It is for this reason that iPhone videos have become virtually a life-saving necessity for Black people during these fraught encounters. As one Black person on Twitter advised after an incident in which a Black teen was falsely accused of stealing a cellphone, "Stay calm and keep the camera steady."

However, given the insidious reality of white social-cultural epistemological privilege, videos are not a guaranteed authenticator for Black knowing. For instance, despite the video that went viral of George Floyd's murder at the knee of police, coupled with other similar videos, not to speak of Black people's testimony that this fatal event reflected a pattern of racist police brutality, one study showed that only 55 percent of the white public compared with 88 percent of Black people believed that

---

53. Leon F. Litwack, *Trouble in Mind: Black Southerners in the Age of Jim Crow* (New York: Knopf, 1998), 253.

54. Vernellia Randall, "Race, Racism, and the Law," August 31, 2019, https://racism.org/about-us/3160-race-racism.

race was a factor. It similarly showed that only 49 percent of whites believed that police are more likely to use force against a Black person than against a white person.[55] Essentially, this study reveals that white epistemological privilege is so profound that it prevents the white public from accepting the truth of Black knowing, even when that truth is right before their eyes.

Just as disconcerting, if not more so, is that even during a period of presumed heightened awareness of racial injustice, Black knowing still could not penetrate the grid of white social-cultural epistemological privilege. It could not break through a conceptual framework of the world that says the way things are is the way they are supposed to be. Nor could it disrupt a pre-vailing social memory that suggests inequitable social condi-tions reflect white resourcefulness and Black incompetence, rather than white supremacist structures. Thus, the Public Reli-gion Research Institute (PRRI) found that even following the 2020 Black Lives Matter summer of protests sparked by racial in-justice, 55 percent of white Americans still maintained that the legacy of slavery and systemic discrimination are non-factors in Black Americans' ability to achieve economic mobility. In fact, this study showed that 44 percent of white Americans believed "discrimination against whites has become as big a problem as discrimination against Black Americans and other minorities." Consistent with these findings, the PRRI study also showed that 50 percent of white Americans "say recent killings of Black men are isolated incidents," as opposed to evidence of systemic racial bias.[56]

---

55. See Ryan Best and Kaleigh Rogers, "Do You Know How Divided White and Black Americans Are on Racism?" June 10, 2020, https://projects. fivethirtyeight.com/racism-polls/.

56. "Summer Unrest over Racial Injustice Moves the Country, but Not Republicans or White Evangelicals," Public Religion Research Institute (PRRI) Staff, August 21, 2020, https://www.prri.org/research/racial-justice-2020-george-floyd/.

An earlier Pew Research Center study showed results similar to the PRRI findings. It found that only 54 percent of white Americans believe racial discrimination has played a significant factor in Black people's inability to get ahead. Fifty percent blame the lack of Black progress on "family instability," while 45 percent blame it on the lack of "good role models." This study also revealed that 60 percent of Black people reported encounters with white people who treated them as if they were "not smart,"[57] suggesting the way in which this white privilege of knowing, wittingly or unwittingly, shapes even mundane encounters between white and Black persons. Borrowing from the words of Isabel Wilkerson, "Every day across America, wherever two or more are gathered, [white social-cultural epistemological privilege] can infect the most ordinary interchanges, catching us off guard, disrupting, and confusing and potentially causing mayhem for everyone."[58]

Overall, what these findings continue to evince is that the reality of white social-cultural epistemological privilege is not just a theoretical construct. It is real. It has truly insinuated itself into the collective conscious of the public. Moreover, in interaction with the anti-Black narrative it has real consequences for Black lives.

Notwithstanding its intrinsic compatibility with an anti-Black narrative, white social-cultural epistemological privilege is itself a construct that sustains a system of domination and thus undermines the possibility for a just democracy. By centering white knowing, it sustains and masks the reality of white supremacy. Thus, it provides white people a foundation for denying the existence of systemic and structural racism. Essen-

---

57. Juliana Menasce Horowitz, Anna Brown, and Kiana Cox, "Race in America 2019," April 9, 2019, https://www.pewsocialtrends.org/2019/04/09/race-in-america-2019/.

58. Isabel Wilkerson, *Caste: The Origins of Our Discontents* (New York: Random House, 2020), 212.

tially, it provides a plausibility structure for denying the reality of white supremacy, and thus for escaping any responsibility for the privileges one gains from it. Again, this very plausibility structure includes the conceptual framework and social memory that form white social-cultural epistemological privilege.

As it happens, no one better exemplifies this plausibility structure of denial than President Trump. "I don't believe it exists," he proclaimed, when asked about systemic racism, particularly as seen in racialized police brutality. When such denial comes from the highest office of the nation it has not only social policy implications but also—perhaps even more insidiously—profound implications for the nation's moral imaginary. Essentially, an authoritative canopy is placed over a "white" knowing that inflects the way a people will perceive justice. In other words, in repudiating the existence of white supremacy, Trump, as a voice of authority, officially bends the arc of justice toward the preservation of white privilege. Thus, white epistemological privilege, effectively masking white supremacy, corrupts and compromises the nation's moral imaginary.

A Compromised Moral Imaginary

In order to appreciate the particular impact of white epistemological privilege in regard to the moral imaginary, we must first understand the inherent problem of epistemological privilege in general. As noted earlier, the defining feature of a social-cultural epistemology of privilege is that it reflects the perspective of the dominant social-cultural group. It elevates the knowledge of those in power, creating a perspective "from above" that sets the standard for knowing, even moral knowing.

To be sure, there is a broad field of philosophical and ethical study that examines the complex realities that constitute what is called "moral epistemology." It is not my intention to engage that discussion. Rather, my intention is to state what is perhaps the obvious: the way in which social-cultural epistemological privilege provides the foundation for various forms of knowledge in the public square, in this instance moral knowledge. Mills puts it this way: "The epistemic desideratum is that the naturalizing and socializing of epistemology should have, as a component, the naturalizing and socializing of *moral* epistemology."[59] In other words, a social-cultural epistemology of privilege inevitably impacts moral knowing. For, if nothing else, it determines whose knowledge has moral efficacy, and this shapes the way in which justice is conceived, if not enacted.

Insofar as it is the knowledge of those who enjoy social-cultural power that is considered valid, then, as we have seen, the knowledge that emerges from the experiences of those on the underside of power is, at best, doubted, and most typically discounted. This means that those who have experienced the profoundest realities of injustice have no voice in shaping what justice looks like. Put another way, the knowledge of those whose very well-being is at stake—in large measure because of the privileges enjoyed by those in power—has no role to play in determining what a just society would look like. Therefore, a form of justice that actually challenges, let alone eliminates, societal inequities is virtually impossible to conceive, especially when those inequities sustain the privileges and power of the dominant social-cultural group.

More specifically, a moral imaginary grounded in an epistemology that normalizes whiteness cannot envision a society that eliminates racial injustice. Such a moral imaginary does not have the capacity to foster social-cultural webs of relationship between white and Black people characterized by equality, mutuality, and reciprocity; such relationships defy notions of inherent white superiority and Black inferiority. Essentially, an America in which those raced Black have equal opportunity to enjoy the same "inalienable rights of life, liberty and the pursuit

---

59. Mills, *Black Rights/White Wrongs*, 58.

of happiness" as those raced white is effectively unachievable within the context of a social-cultural epistemology of privilege that masks white supremacy. We should be reminded that even the man who wrote this vision of equality into the Declaration of Independence, Thomas Jefferson, recognized its impossibility when he declared, with certainty, that "the two races, equally free, cannot live in the same government."[60]

In the final analysis, the ultimate impact of white social-cultural epistemological privilege is that it desensitizes people to "social oppression and the attempt to reduce and ultimately eliminate that oppression."[61] It does not provide the impetus to take seriously, or even listen to, the experiences of people on the social-cultural "bottom" of society. The presumption is that there is nothing worth knowing that they could provide. There-fore, not only are they ignored but the unjust conditions that shape their lives are overlooked. It is assumed that "nothing good can come from" the places of the "unprivileged." This is how social-cultural epistemological privilege holds the moral imaginary captive. There is nothing that points to this captivity more than the persistent presence of Confederate monuments on the public square.

Confederate Monuments as Moral Signifiers

On June 17, 2015, nine Black people, including the church pas-tor, were killed by a young white man during a Bible study at Emanuel A.M.E. in Charleston, South Carolina. The young man who carried out this massacre was a white supremacist whose reported goal was to initiate a race war. Pictures on social media showed him surrounded by the Confederate flag and other white supremacist symbols. In response, many cities and states began taking down or quietly removing Confederate statues,

---

60. *Autobiography of Thomas Jefferson, 1743–1790*, Kindle edition, 48.

61. Mills, *Black Rights/White Wrongs*, 58.

flags, and other memorials. Even the Confederate flag that flew on the statehouse grounds of South Carolina, the first state to secede from the Union, was taken down, as well as the one that stood on the Capitol grounds in Montgomery, Alabama, the former capital of the Confederacy.

After witnessing such racial hatred legitimated by a Confederate flag, it seemed that the nation had perhaps turned a corner in recognizing that Confederate symbols were anathema to America's vision for itself, at least to the vision articulated in the Declaration of Independence. And yet, five years after the Charleston massacre, according to an SPLC report, while 114 Confederate symbols had been removed, another 1,747 still stood, including 780 monuments. In fact, laws in various former Confederate states prohibit these monuments from being taken down.[62]

Furthermore, after the riot in Charlottesville to protect the Robert E. Lee monument, a riot that resulted in the death of thirty-two-year-old Heather Heyer, and after a summer of racial justice protests, the PPRI study found that a majority of white Americans, 57 percent, still believe the Confederate flag is a symbol of Southern pride, not racism. With regard to the Confederate monuments, the number of white Americans who view them as representing Southern pride is even higher, at 68 percent. Perhaps needless to say, these numbers are significantly different when it comes to Black Americans, who responded at 16 and 28 percent, respectively, to the above questions.

As has been shown in this chapter, these monuments are not innocuous representations of "Southern pride." They are decided symbols of white supremacy. The various protests—sometimes violent, often led by white supremacists—that erupt when monuments are removed attest to their meaning. These monuments stand as veritable "dog whistles" across time to white supremacists, telling them that their cause is not lost.

---

62. See "Whose Heritage? Public Symbols of the Confederacy."

What President Trump shamelessly put into words to white supremacists as he refused to condemn one such group during a 2020 presidential debate, the Confederate monuments say by their very presence on the public square: "Stand back and stand by."[63] As long as they remain part of the public landscape, they witness to a nation that is undecided regarding the kind of nation it wants to be. Will this be a nation that continues the legacy of a slaveholding nation? Or will this be a nation that lives into a vision in which the inalienable rights of all people are protected? When all is said and done, these monuments tell the story of a nation that has consistently struggled to decide if its democratic vision is more rhetoric than reality. Hence, they provide hope for those who cling to this nation's white supremacist identity. They suggest a nation that is always on the verge of a civil war, one that can erupt with little provocation.

Back to the Conversation

"Black folks should seriously consider packing our bags.... We are headed for another Civil War."

This text from my son, which continued our conversation about Confederate monuments, points to the significance of these monuments as conceptual symbols and symbols of social memory serving to substantiate a white supremacist concept of the world and the nation. As my son rightly understood, inasmuch as these monuments remain in the public square, they signal a civil war still to be fought—the end result leaving Black lives in further peril, especially—as we have seen—under the leadership of a president who vowed to "Make America Great Again."

---

63. "Donald Trump Refuses to Condemn White Supremacists at Presidential Debate," *The Guardian*, September 29, 2020, https://www.theguardian.com/us-news/2020/sep/29/trump-proud-boys-debate-president-refuses-condemn-white-supremacists.

At the time of my son's text, I did not realize how close the nation was to civil war. And then it happened. On January 6, 2021, at the very moment when Congress was due to certify the electoral victory of President-Elect Joe Biden and Vice President-Elect Kamala Harris, supporters of the "Make America Great Again" vision, incited by their leader, stormed Congress. Members of this mob were seen carrying Confederate flags alongside Trump banners. These Confederate flags were proudly carried down the halls of the congressional buildings and even into the chambers. Others in the mob wore sweatshirts emblazoned with "Camp Auschwitz," along with other white supremacist paraphernalia. A noose hung on a gallows, erected in front of the west side of the Capitol where the insurrectionists had gathered.[64] Perhaps worse yet was the fact that these mostly white insurrectionists were not met with the kind of militarized police enforcement that is regularly deployed against Black Lives Matter protesters on the public square for justice. In fact, these insurrectionists were able to stop legislative work, send members of Congress fleeing into hiding, trash the halls of Congress, break windows, ram through doors, leave five people dead—including a police officer—and walk out virtually unmolested.

Lynda Williams, president of the National Organization of Black Law Enforcement Executives (NOBLE), articulated well what Black people across America felt as they watched the way in which the violent white mob was treated play out in stark contrast to the way in which peaceful Black protesters have been treated. She said: "If those protesters [at the U.S. Capitol] were Black and brown there would have been a bloodbath."[65] "But

---

64. Stephanie K. Baer, "Trump Supporters Who Attempted the Coup at the US Capitol Flaunted Racist and Hateful Symbols," *Buzzfeed*, January 6, 2021, https://www.buzzfeednews.com/article/skbaer/trump-supporters-racist-symbols-capitol-assault.

65. CNN, "Racial Justice Leaders Are Reeling from the 'Hypocrisy' in the Police Response to the US Capitol Riots," June 8, 2020, https://abc17news.

there's one question I can't shake," former First Lady Michelle Obama tweeted: "What if those rioters look like the folks who go to Ebenezer Baptist Church every Sunday? What would have been different? I think we all know the answer to that."[66] Even President-Elect Joe Biden recognized this, in comments that he made when he addressed the nation: "No one can tell me that if it had been a group of Black Lives Matter protesters yesterday that they wouldn't have been treated very differently than the mob that stormed the Capitol. We all know that's true—and it's unacceptable."[67]

Alicia Garza, co-founder of Black Lives Matter, perhaps summed it up best when she observed:

> I think what the events of this week have shown us is that there have always been multiple Americas.... There's been an America that we read about in history books—a romantic America that is made of fairy tales. And then there's America that some of us live in—an America where the rules have been rigged against us for a very long time.
>
> It's an America where the rules around race and gender and class are fundamental, and they shape and impact people's everyday lives. It's also an America where we function under a particular sense of amnesia.[68]

The message writ large to Black America was that Black lives don't matter because the Black story, Black knowing, don't matter.

com/news/national-world/2021/01/08/racial-justice-leaders-are-reeling-from-the-hypocrisy-in-the-police-response-to-the-us-capitol-riots/.

66. See https://twitter.com/MichelleObama/status/1347284244763127810/photo/1.

67. See https://www.npr.org/2021/01/07/954568499/protests-inwhite-and-black-and-the-different-response-of-law-enforcement.

68. See https://abc17news.com/news/national-world/2021/01/08/racial-justice-leaders-are-reeling-from-the-hypocrisy-in-the-police-response-to-the-us-capitol-riots/.

The Black story to bring America closer to its vision of a just democracy is the story that is erased from America's social memory. It is the one deemed by President Trump as "un-American." If the story a nation writes is the story it becomes, then the civil war insurrection at the Capitol was telling us what this nation has become. For if it told us nothing else, it proclaimed that even as Trump and his vision to "Make America Great Again" were defeated, the nation itself was still divided regarding what kind of nation it ultimately wanted to become.

There is no getting around it. The endurance of Confederate symbols and monuments signal that this nation's moral imaginary has made peace with white supremacy. The fact that in 2016 America elected a clear white supremacist as president was already evidence of that. Thus, with little provocation, white supremacy erupted into the halls of Congress to protect the cause that Confederate monuments represent. And so, my son is right: as long as the Confederate monuments have a place in this country, Black lives will never be truly safe.

What then are we to do? How are we ever to free our landscape from these statuary symbols standing guard over white supremacy? Here again, Tillich's comments on symbols are helpful. He reminds us that symbols are not arbitrary. "They grow," he says, "out of the individual or collective unconscious and cannot function without being accepted by the unconscious dimension of our being." In short, he says, "they grow when the situation is ripe for them, and they die when the situation changes."[69]

The bottom line is this: Confederate monuments do indeed tell us something about our nation. That they remain on the public square reveals the deep meaning they still hold. "The situation" in the nation remains "ripe for them." To reiterate, these monuments reveal a nation whose moral imaginary is captive to a white supremacist vision of society, if not of the world. And

---

69. Tillich, *Dynamics of Faith*, 49.

thus, that these monuments are seen as acceptable features on the public square indicates that this nation cannot yet open itself to hold a vision of Black equality and thus to become a nation where Black lives truly matter. In order for the monuments to be removed from the nation's landscape, therefore, the situation must change. This means that the moral imaginary must be freed from its captivity to a white supremacist way of knowing. And how is that to happen?

Inasmuch as faith is about partnering with God to mend an unjust earth, and thus to move us to a more just future, then faith communities, by definition, are accountable to that future. It is a future where all people will be treated as sacred beings, free from dehumanizing fetters. This is a future to which the soul of this nation calls us. It is faith leaders, therefore, who must help the nation hear that call, so that it can live into its better angels. The faith community must help the nation forge a different social memory by reaching back to those stories in which people gave their lives—not to a white supremacist cause, but to enact the vision toward which the Declaration of Independence pointed. If nothing else, faith communities must embody and show forth an alternative moral vision in witness to the fact that there is a possibility beyond a moral imaginary that equates white privilege with justice.

It is in this way that faith leaders will help free the moral imaginary of this nation from its captivity to a white supremacist worldview. And, it is only when this happens that Confederate monuments will be eradicated from the nation's landscape. For then, the nation's moral imaginary will no longer be able to tolerate them. The situation will no longer "be ripe" for them.

Once again clinging to the hope of faith, I texted my son back: "I'm not ready to pack my bags yet...but we'll see."

3

It's about the Good White Christians

"I like what she had to say, but where were all those white ministers when it was just Black people out there protesting? Now they come out to defend a church from Trump? Why didn't they defend Black people from him?"

This was my son's response after Mariann Edgar Budde, the Episcopal bishop of the Diocese of Washington, DC, expressed "outrage" at President Trump's photo-op in front of St. John's Episcopal Church on June 1, 2020. Trump staged this photo-op in defiance of Black Lives Matter protests in Washington and around the country triggered by the murder of George Floyd. Bishop Budde seethed at the way in which peaceful protesters in Lafayette Park had been attacked with tear gas, flash grenades, and rubber bullets to clear a path for the president to pose with a Bible in front of the church. She said: "I am the bishop of the Episcopal Diocese of Washington and was not given even a courtesy call, that they would be clearing [the area] with tear gas so they could use one of our churches as a prop."[1] Bishop Budde

---

1. Michelle Boorstein and Sarah Pulliam Bailey, "Episcopal Bishop on President Trump: 'Everything He Has Said and Done Is to Inflame Violence,'" *Washington Post*, June 1, 2020, https://www.washingtonpost.com/religion/

also expressed her "outrage" at Trump's misuse, if not blaspheming of religious symbols, including the Bible. She declared:

> I am outraged. The President did not pray when he came to St. John's, nor…did he acknowledge the agony of our country right now. And in particular, that of the people of color in our nation, who wonder if anyone ever—anyone in public power will ever acknowledge their sacred words. And who are rightfully demanding an end to 400 years of systemic racism and white supremacy in our country. And I just want the world to know, that we in the diocese of Washington, following Jesus and his way of love…we distance ourselves from the incendiary language of this President. We follow someone who lived a life of nonviolence and sacrificial love. We align ourselves with those seeking justice for the death of George Floyd and countless others. And I just can't believe what my eyes have seen.[2]

While I remain proud of my bishop for speaking out that day, my son's words were also haunting. Where have been the bold, loud, and passionate voices of white Christian leaders like Bishop Budde as Black bodies have been routinely desecrated by white racism? Many did join in the protests triggered by the George Floyd video, but where were they before that video? Where was their outrage following the murders of Tamir Rice, Philando Castile, John Crawford, Atatiana Jefferson, and numerous others? Where were the white Christian voices as the virus of white supremacist anti-Black injustice disproportionately trapped Black lives in the crucifying realities of poverty? Black

---

bishop-budde-trump-church/2020/06/01/20ca70f8-a466-11ea-b619-3f9133bbb482_story.html.

2. Paul Leblanc, "Bishop at DC Church Outraged by Trump Visit: 'I just Can't Believe What My Eyes Have Seen,'" CNN, June 2, 2020, https://www.cnn.com/2020/06/01/politics/cnntv-bishop-trump-photo-op/index.html.

communities had long suffered from the co-morbidities that left them particularly vulnerable to the ravages of COVID-19. Where were the voices of white Christians before COVID-19 laid bare these racialized co-morbidities? My son's text took me back to another time when I was waiting to hear from white faith leaders in my own Episcopal tradition, but was left waiting.

On June 13, 2013, a six-woman jury in Florida acquitted the murderer of Trayvon Martin, the seventeen-year-old African American youth who was shot by a self-appointed neighborhood watchman.[3] In doing so, they all but confirmed the 1857 Dred Scott decision by the Supreme Court, which validated the nation's white supremacist identity by asserting that Black people had "no rights which the white man was bound to respect."

On June 25, just twelve days after the acquittal of Trayvon's killer, the Supreme Court ruling in the *Shelby v. Holder* case practically eviscerated the 1965 Voting Rights Act, which provided protections to ensure that Black people had equal access to the ballot, free of intimidation. The *Shelby* ruling eliminated the provision in the Voting Rights Act that compelled states with a historical pattern of suppressing and intimidating the Black vote to obtain federal approval before making changes in voting requirements or procedures. In effect, the Supreme Court ruling essentially affirmed that the right to vote was a privilege of whiteness. The immediate and inevitable consequence was a record number of complaints and cases brought before the courts as states gerrymandered, purged voting rolls, closed polling places, and employed other tactics with "surgical precision" to disenfranchise Black voters.[4] This ruling, in fact, laid the foundation for the state of Georgia to implement twenty-first-

---

3. See my previous book, *Stand Your Ground: Black Bodies and the Justice of God* (Maryknoll, NY: Orbis Books, 2015).

4. United States Court of Appeal for the Fourth Circuit No. 16-1468, https://electionlawblog.org/wp-content/uploads/nc-4th.pdf.

century Jim Crow voting restrictions following the 2020 election. These restrictions included making it a felony to provide food or water to people waiting in line to vote. President Biden said that Georgia's twenty-first-century voting restrictions "make Jim Crow look like Jim Eagle."[5]

In the span of twelve days in the summer of 2013, two judicial decisions sent a resounding message to the Black community: America's democracy is not meant for you.

As disturbed as I was by these two judicial actions, which actually affirmed the constitutionality of white supremacy, no doubt in keeping with the Framers' original intent, what struck me most was the virtual silence from presumably "good" white Christians. I was most distressed by the resounding quiet from the church where I was soon to become canon theologian, the Washington National Cathedral. After all, as the nation's Cathedral it had not shied away from "controversial social justice issues" before. It was a leading voice in the struggle for "commonsense" gun control laws as well as the movement for LGBTQ rights. But racial justice seemed to be a different matter altogether. There was something that prevented the church from wading into those waters.

This became most obvious to me after the Cathedral held a service of celebration, and rightly so, for the June 26, 2013, Supreme Court rulings regarding LGBTQ rights. The rulings struck down the Defense of Marriage Act and California's Proposition 8, thus opening the door for same-gendered marriages throughout the country. As celebratory as this service was, the fact that the Cathedral had uttered hardly a whimpering lament about the devastating voting rights decision that

---

5. Seung Min Kim, "Biden Attacks New Georgia Voting Law as 'Jim Crow,'" *Washington Post*, March 26, 2021. https://www. washingtonpost.com/politics/biden-georgia-law-jim-crow/2021/03/26/35383056-8e40-11eb-a730-1b4ed9656258_story.html.

the Court had delivered only a day earlier stood out. The silence of these good white Christians when it came to race was
palpable. Was this the silence, I wondered, that had allowed
the Washington National Cathedral to display for over sixty
years (before they were removed in 2017) stained-glass windows honoring two men who fought for slavery? I had not
known about the presence of these windows, but others did
know—and yet they had remained silent. The words of Martin
Luther King Jr. echoed in my ears: "The ultimate tragedy is not
the oppression and cruelty by the bad people but the silence
over that by the good people."[6] How was I to understand such
silence from this body of white Christians whom I knew to be
ostensibly "good people" in terms of their commitments to social justice? In the words of King, these were people of "genuine good will."[7]

Even though they were reluctant to speak out boldly when
it came to racial justice, I was all but certain that this silence was
not the same as that of white "Christians" who vociferously justified slavery. It was not even the legacy of those who fought
against slavery, yet supported notions of Black inferiority. Neither did this silence seem to reflect the legacy of evangelical
leaders like Cotton Mather, who believed slavery to be a divinely ordained "blessing," or George Whitefield, who proclaimed no difference between white souls and Black souls, who
advocated for more humane treatment of the enslaved (as if
there was a way for chattel slavery to be humane), and who
termed some slave owners "Monsters of Barbarity," yet did not
criticize the institution itself and was himself a slaveholder. I
knew also that it did not reflect the silence of a person like Con-
gregationalist minister Josiah Strong, who argued that America

---

6. Martin Luther King Jr., "Letter from a Birmingham Jail," April 16,
1963, https://kinginstitute.stanford.edu/sites/mlk/files/letterfrombirmingham_
wwcw_0.pdf.

7. King, "Letter from a Birmingham Jail."

was called to reflect a "pure spiritual Christianity," exemplified by the Anglo-Saxon race. And, to be sure, the silence of these "good people" did not reflect the legacy of the vilest forms of religious racism reflected in one such as Charles Carroll, who proclaimed in his popular book of the same name, "Negro a Beast." Nor did it reflect the views of my Episcopal denomination's eighth presiding bishop, John Henry Hopkins, who in 1863 published the *Bible View of Slavery* and proclaimed that any "candid observer agrees that the negro is happier and better as a slave than as a free man, and no individual belonging to the Anglo-Saxon stock would acknowledge that the intellect of the negro is equal to his own."

These historical responses to racial injustice each reflected a fundamental belief in the innate inferiority of Black people, if not also the theological acceptability of chattel slavery and white supremacy. In fact, these responses were not indicative of a silence on matters of racial injustice. Rather, they were vociferous in espousing an unapologetically racist version of Christianity. The legacy of this vociferous tradition has not gone away.

I will never forget my appearance on C-SPAN's Bill Scanlon call-in show. I was invited to speak about an article I had written on evangelism and white supremacy. During the call-in segment, a man called ostensibly to proclaim that "God loves everybody." Yet, in making this proclamation the caller made sure to explain that "Black people were created on the sixth day," while "God created Adam and Eve, on the seventh day." The caller went on to describe Adam and Eve as a people who were "able to show blush... to show red in the face."[8] As I listened to him recite his erroneous version of the Genesis creation narrative as well as his views on skin color, my thoughts raced back to Charles Carroll's *The Negro a Beast*. The caller's intent

---

8. "Reverend Kelly Brown Douglas on Evangelicalism and Race," *Washington Journal*, April 21, 2018, https://www.c-span.org/video/?444310-5/washington-journal-reverend-kelly-brown-douglas-discusses-evangelicalism-race.

was clear. He was suggesting that while God may love everybody, Black people were among the nonhuman animals (that is, beasts) created on what he called "the sixth day." Coupled with the fact that he was suggesting that a white complexion was more fitting for the "dust" from which humans were created, this argument was an attempt to place Black people outside the creation of humans. As if to apologize for what he knew to be a racist rendering of the creation narrative, the caller added, "That's just the way it is."[9]

Just as white supremacy has not disappeared, neither has the religion that fosters and legitimates it. As white supremacy has transformed itself throughout the nation's history to reflect the customs and "constraints of the time," so too have white supremacist versions of Christianity. In our own time, these racist renderings of Christianity have simply adapted to twenty-first-century cultural mores and political sensibilities, thereby manifesting in ways perhaps more subtle than the caller's proclamation concerning creation, but no less blatant. We see this, for instance, in white Christian support for the "Make America Great Again" vision.

Data from the 2016 elections which resulted in a Trump presidency reveal that over 80 percent of white evangelical Protestants, 60 percent of white Catholics, and more than 50 percent of non-evangelical white Protestants supported his vision for the nation.[10] Theological and religious scholars have studied the significance of the enormous white evangelical support for

---

9. "Reverend Kelly Brown Douglas on Evangelicalism and Race."

10. See Philip Bump, "A Third of Trump's Support in 2016 Came from Evangelicals—and He Hasn't Lost Them Yet," *Washington Post*, June 5, 2020, https://www.washingtonpost.com/politics/2020/06/05/third-trumps-support-2016-came-evangelicals-and-he-hasnt-lost-them-yet/. See also Jessica Martinez and Gregory A. Smith, "How the Faithful Voted: A Preliminary 2016 Analysis," November 9, 2016, https://www.pewresearch.org/fact-tank/2016/11/09/how-the-faithful-voted-a-preliminary-2016-analysis/.

Trump. They have sought to understand how a Christian community that customarily proclaims "traditional family values" could support a twice-divorced candidate with numerous allegations of adulterous behavior and sexual misconduct lodged against him. What they have not focused on is the fact that, evangelical or not, the majority of white Christians support and affirm a vision that defies the central message of the Christian gospel: God's promise of a just future where every person's sacred humanity is respected.

White Christian support of Trump's candidacy was not incidental; rather, it reflects deep-seated values. This has been made evident in various surveys conducted by the Public Religion and Research Institute (PRRI).

One such PRRI survey showed that approximately two-thirds of all white Christians, or 72 percent of white Protestant evangelicals and 62 percent of non-evangelical white Protestants and white Catholics, "believe that the American way of life needs protecting" from those they perceive to be corrupting influences, such as immigrants of color and Muslims. Hence, two-thirds of white Christians, with similar percentages among white evangelicals and white non-evangelicals, support a Muslim ban and erecting a wall on the southern U.S. border.

The support of white Christians for these policies corresponds to their support of Trump's vision to "Make America Great Again." To reiterate, in explaining this vision, Trump promulgated the notion that immigrants of color are, on the whole, threats to "the American way of life." Allowing that some (he "assumes") "are good people," Trump repeatedly declared that Mexican immigrants "are not our friends," accusing them of bringing drugs and crime into the country, as well as being "rapists."[11] His overall message was clear: if America was

---

11. Katie Reilly, "Here Are All the Times Donald Trump Insulted Mexico," *Time*, August 31, 2016, https://time.com/4473972/donald-trump-mexico-meeting-insult/.

going to be "great again," it had to protect itself from the dangerous people, whom he sometimes called "animals," attempting to cross the southern border. "You wouldn't believe how bad these people are. These aren't people, these are animals," Trump ranted.[12] Further revealing the white supremacist nature of the MAGA vision, Trump advocated restricting, if not banning, immigrants from Africa and other so-called "shithole countries," while encouraging immigrants from countries such as Norway[13] To say the least, these policies were steeped in white supremacist ideological assumptions about the superiority of white people to people of color. For white Christians to support such a vision and its concomitant policies reflects an ongoing legacy of religious racism. Moreover, views like these lend themselves to a version of Christian nationalism as expressed by former U.S. Attorney General Jeff Sessions's "Christian" defense of bigoted immigration policies.

In justifying the treatment of immigrants and refugees as criminals, Sessions cited a line from the Pauline letter to the Romans (13:1): "Let everyone be subject to the governing authorities, for there is no authority except that which God has established . . . ," as if to equate "Christian" (notably white Christian) identity with what it means to be American.[14] The fact is that Christian support of the MAGA vision provides religious

12. Julie Hirschfeld Davis, "Trump Calls Some Unauthorized Immigrants 'Animals' in Rant," *New York Times*, May 16, 2018, https://www.nytimes.com/2018/05/16/us/politics/trump-undocumented-immigrants-animals.html.

13. Josh Dawsey, "Trump Derides Protections for Immigrants from 'Shithole' Countries," *Washington Post*, January 12, 2018, https://www.washingtonpost.com/politics/trump-attacks-protections-for-immigrants-from-shithole-countries-in-oval-office-meeting/2018/01/11/bfc0725c-f711-11e7-91af-31ac729add94_story.html.

14. Emily McFarlan Miller and Yonat Shimron, "Why Is Jeff Sessions Quoting Romans 13 and Why is the Bible Verse So Often Invoked?" *Religion News Service*, June 16, 2018, https://www.usatoday.com/story/news/2018/06/16/jeff-sessions-bible-romans-13-trump-immigration-policy/707749002/.

cover, if not legitimation, for white supremacy—hence perpetu-ating the legacy of racist Christian beliefs espoused by persons such as Josiah Strong, Charles Carroll, and others. White Chris-tian denials of systemic and structural racism further evince this legacy.

Recent surveys have shown that white Christians tend to as-sume that Black people use racism to justify their lack of progress rather than take responsibility for it themselves. A 2018 PPRI survey specifically showed that more than three quarters of white Christians "believe that racial minorities use racism as an excuse for economic inequalities more than they should." This study also revealed that fewer than 40 percent of white Christians believe that the legacy of slavery has impacted Black social-economic progress. PRRI reports that "more than six in ten white Christians overall *disagree* with this basic statement: 'Generations of slavery and discrimination have created condi-tions that make it difficult for Blacks to work their way out of the lower class.'"[15]

A more recent PRRI survey taken following the 2020 Black Lives Matter protests saw little change in the overall attitudes of white Christians in this regard.[16] It is also worth recalling the PEW study mentioned in the previous chapter showing results similar to these PRRI findings.[17] Essentially, these findings sup-port Ibram Kendi's observation that "Americans have long been trained to see the deficiencies of people rather than policies," es-pecially when it comes to Black people.

---

15. Robert P. Jones, *White Too Long: The Legacy of White Supremacy in American Christianity* (New York: Simon and Schuster, 2020), 162.

16. "Summer Unrest over Racial Injustice Moves the Country, but Not Republicans or White Evangelicals," PRRI, August 21, 2020, https://www.prri.org/research/racial-justice-2020-george-floyd/.

17. Juliana Menasce Horowitz, Anna Brown, and Kiana Cox, "Race in America 2019," April 9, 2019, https://www.pewsocialtrends.org/2019/04/09/race-in-america-2019/.

That Black people are generally blamed for their lack of success while white people are typically lauded for their resourcefulness and good work ethic is reminiscent of the white supremacist/anti-Black claim that Black people lack the intellectual capacity or even the requisite work ethic to succeed. When white Christians tacitly support such a belief by declaring that Black people play the racism card as an excuse for their own shortcomings, innate or otherwise, they virtually echo Bishop Hopkins's white supremacist/anti-Black assertions that Black people are intellectually inferior to "Anglo-Saxons."

That the legacy of Christian religious racism resounds in twenty-first America is indisputable, even as it masks itself in the rhetoric of and policies to "Make America Great Again." The power of this legacy is demonstrated in findings which reveal that, compared to religiously unaffiliated whites, white Christians, especially those who attend church regularly, are most likely to support the "Make America Great Again" vision and policies.

We see one expression of this in the fact that, as mentioned in the previous chapter, according to PRRI: "White Christian groups are most likely to view Confederate monuments as symbols of Southern pride rather than racism, including strong majorities of white evangelical Protestants (86%), white Catholics (78%), and white mainline Protestants (70%)." Again, it is notable that only 45 percent of the religiously unaffiliated—that is, non-Christian white Americans—believe such symbols are not racist.[18]

These overall findings led religious scholar and founder of PRRI Robert Jones to starkly conclude: "If you were recruiting for a white supremacist cause on a Sunday morning, you'd likely have more success hanging out in the parking lot of an av-

---

18. See "Summer Unrest over Racial Injustice Moves the Country, but Not Republicans or White Evangelicals."

erage white Christian church—evangelical Protestant, mainline
Protestant, or Catholic—than approaching whites sitting out
services at the local coffee shop."[19]

Undoubtedly there are complex cultural and political dynamics at play which account for the findings behind Jones's
observation. Perhaps, for instance, it is the case that those who
identify as politically liberal or progressive tend not to affiliate
with institutionalized religion, but are otherwise deeply spiritual. Pew studies on the U.S. religious landscape suggest this to
be the case.[20] To be sure, the relationship between a person's political philosophy and his or her affiliation with institutionalized religion deserves further exploration, which goes beyond
the scope of this discussion. The relevant point here is that a vibrant legacy of Christian religious racism continues to thrive.
This clearly signals that there is something about Christianity's
theological architecture that makes it at least vulnerable to
being used in oppressive ways—as evident throughout Christian history itself. Specifically, there are aspects of Christianity
which make it susceptible to white racist distortions and thus
render Christianity potentially toxic when it comes to white supremacist ideology.[21] It was no doubt such a recognition that led
Frederick Douglass to proclaim that being enslaved by a religious master was the worst calamity of all. In his words, "Were
I to be again reduced to the chains of slavery, next to that enslavement, I should regard being the slave of a religious master
the greatest calamity that could befall me. For of all slaveholders with whom I have ever met, religious slaveholders are the
worst. I have found them the meanest and basest, the most

---

19. Jones, *White Too Long*, 185.

20. See https://www.pewforum.org/religious-landscape-study/religious-
denomination/spiritual-but-not-religious/.

21. I have expanded upon this in *What's Faith Got to Do with It? Black Bodies and Christian Souls* (Maryknoll, NY: Orbis Books, 2005).

cruel and cowardly of all others."[22] Even with that said, however, Douglass made a distinction between slaveholding religion and Christianity. He said, "What I have said respecting and against religion, I mean strictly to apply to the *slaveholding religion* of this land, and with no possible reference to Christianity proper; for, between the Christianity of this land, and the Christianity of Christ, I recognize the widest possible difference."[23] Howard Thurman made a similar distinction as he differentiated between a prevailing expression of Christianity that maintained the legacy of slavery on the one hand and the religion of Jesus on the other.[24] And indeed, such a distinction is implied in my son's wondering where the voices of white Christians like Bishop Budde's were before the absurd and atrocious displays of white supremacy grabbed the media spotlight.

The silence my son was pointing to, as well as that which I encountered at the Washington National Cathedral, did not reflect a theological pattern that supports the inherent inequality of people or the notion that God created some people, that is, Black people, to be enslaved by another people. This was evident in Bishop Budde's declaration of solidarity "with those seeking justice for the death of George Floyd and countless others." It is also evident in the ongoing social justice work of the Washington National Cathedral. These "silent" white Christians are not like those "Christians" who were perhaps among the white supremacists storming the halls of Congress to "Stop the Steal" and "Make America Great Again." They do not represent the legacy of slaveholding Christianity or religious racism.

---

22. *Narrative of the Life of Frederick Douglass*, in *The Classic Slave Narratives*, edited with an introduction by Henry Louis Gates Jr. (New York: Mentor Books, 1987), 301–2.

23. *Narrative of the Life of Frederick Douglass*, 326.

24. Howard Thurman, *Jesus and the Disinherited* (Richmond, IN: Friends United Press, 1981), 13ff.

As my son's question continued to replay in my head, and as I searched for answers, I reflected on my own Episcopal Church's institutional response to chattel slavery. Unlike the Baptist, Methodist, and Presbyterian denominations, which split over slavery, the Episcopal Church did not split into northern and southern branches. That it met as two separate bodies during the Civil War (the General Convention of the Protestant Episcopal Church in the United States of America and the General Council of the Confederate States of America) was more a matter of practical necessity than it was a disagreement over the morality of slavery. Instead, as a denomination it remained "aloof" and virtually silent about slavery as a theological or moral issue. Nevertheless, such silence created a comfortable space for slaveholders, thereby gaining for the denomination its well-earned reputation as a church of wealthy slaveholders.

Some one hundred years after the Civil War, two Episcopal bishops joined six other faith leaders during the 1963 Birmingham civil rights struggle in issuing "A Call for Unity." They warned against participation in the "extreme measures" of Martin Luther King Jr. to end segregation and other forms of racial injustice in that city, deeming his actions divisive and a catalyst for "hatred and violence." In the end, they urged the "Negro community to withdraw support from these demonstrations, and to unite locally in working peacefully for a better Birmingham." Their call for unity seemed to reflect the Episcopal Church's lack of "indignation" regarding slavery.

As resoundingly loud as their message was about the violent disruption they believed King was causing, they were unashamedly silent regarding the segregationist anti-Black divisions and white supremacist violence devastating Black lives. The "call" from this group of interfaith religious leaders prompted King to write his famous "Letter from a Birmingham Jail." In it he recognized that these leaders "fail[ed] to express a similar concern for the conditions that brought about the demonstrations." He further decried faith leaders who "have remained silent behind the anesthetizing security of stained-glass windows."[25]

What was behind this legacy of silence? I found myself asking the question that Howard Thurman had asked decades before: "Why is it that [white] Christianity seems impotent to deal radically, and therefore, effectively, with the issues of discrimination and injustice on the basis of race, religion and national origin?"[26] It cannot be said enough that even as good white Christians are silent, the MAGA Christians are not. Hence, given the pronounced legacy of Christian religious racism, the silence of the "good white Christians" is even more conspicuous, if not troubling. Such silence, as King would say, is the "ultimate tragedy" in a society where Black lives do not matter. And so it was urgent for me, especially as a member of a white denomination with a history of such silence, to try to understand what was behind the silence of good white Christians. I had to answer my son's question.

Systematic theologian Willie Jennings points to the complex ways in which whiteness represents a "diseased" social imagination that distorts the Christian "theological imagination." He argues that Christian theology made adjustments with the imperialistic/colonial project that overspread the lands of non-white peoples around the globe. Moreover, he states that Christianity easily assimilated to the "New World" that resulted from this white expansionist project. Thus, he says, Christianity began to "enfold" itself inside a racialized existence defined by whiteness. Jennings essentially argues that the Christian church established its presence within a white supremacist social-cultural eco-system, finding a way to accom-

---

25. King, "Letter from a Birmingham Jail," April 16, 1963, https://king institute.stanford.edu/sites/mlk/files/letterfrombirmingham_wwcw_0.pdf.

26. Thurman, *Jesus and the Disinherited*, 7.

modate and make peace with it, signaling a distorted theological imagination.

Jennings is right to point to the way in which whiteness, as it signals white supremacist ideology and assumptions, has no doubt led to a distorted theological imagination. This is most clearly evident in slaveholding religion and religious racism as well as their continuing legacy. But again, the silence of good white Christians is not explained by this legacy, or even by overt white supremacist values for that matter. There is something other than the toxic combination that is white supremacist values and Christianity's theological architecture that results in an almost predictable silence when it comes to good white Christian responses to various racial justice issues. What I have come to recognize is that this silence reflects the conceptual limitations inherent in the white gaze. Before looking at this more specifically, let us be reminded of what is meant by the white gaze.

The white gaze defines social-cultural epistemological privilege. It denotes a white way of knowing that has become normative in determining the "truth" regarding the nation's story as well as social experiences and reality. Overall, this is a gaze that reflects not only the interests but also the nature of white supremacy itself. Just as white supremacy is oppositional, so too is the white gaze. Specifically, white supremacy exists only in subjugating, dominating, and deadly opposition to that which is non-white. In like manner, the white gaze views the world and reality through an either/or oppositional lens in which whiteness is the standard for truth and justice, while that which is non-white is seen as fallacious and unjust. This brings us to a perceptual flaw of the white gaze that contributes to white Christian silence regarding racial justice.

In essence, the white gaze represents an oppositional binary that shapes the way one perceives and interprets reality and, by extension, adjudicates justice. It is literally and figuratively a white/Black dichotomous meta-prism through which one sees the world. This a prism through which a white vantage point is revered and a Black vantage point vilified. There is no room for "gray" areas or paradoxes. The white gaze is unable to apprehend paradoxical perceptions of reality.

Reflecting its Greek roots, a paradox (*para* + *doxa* = against belief) suggests an apparent contradiction, or even a logical absurdity. As such, a paradox defies an either/or lens. It defies oppositional binary knowing and perceiving. A paradox holds what may seem to be contradictory in complementary relationship. A paradoxical prism permits a both/and approach to seeing the world. It recognizes the "gray" areas. In fact, it finds meaning in the "gray." Simply put, it is in the paradox itself that meaning is found. This kind of paradoxical meaning eludes a white gaze. To repeat, an oppositional binary is limited; it simply cannot accommodate a paradox. Thus, it is virtually impossible for a way of seeing defined by an oppositional binary to grasp the paradoxes of reality. This presents a particular problem for Christians who wittingly or unwittingly see through a white gaze, for Christianity's defining core is itself a paradox: a crucified Christ.

The meaning of the paradox that is the incarnation—Jesus as the divine/human encounter—is found fully in Jesus's crucifixion. The cross, as Christianity's central symbol, points to the paradoxical nature of the Christian God. Inasmuch as a white gaze inhibits one's ability to apprehend the meaning that emerges from paradoxical realities, it hinders one from appreciating the meaning and complexities of God's incarnate revelation. In other words, the white gaze cannot readily hold—if it can hold at all—theological paradoxes. This has implications for the way in which good white Christians view particular issues that impact their responses to the struggle for racial justice.

Making the white gaze even more problematic, if not more pronounced when it comes to Christianity, and hence the quest for racial justice, is that this gaze reflects the perspective of the dominant social/cultural group—that is, the powerful class. However, the meaning of God's incarnate revelation, as the cross makes abundantly clear, is that the cross is best understood from the vantage point of the subjugated, those on the underside of power—the "disinherited" as Thurman would say. The Apostle Paul put it this way in his Letter to the Corinthians, "God chose the weak things of the world to shame the strong." One must be able to grasp this paradox if one is to truly understand the meaning of God's revelation.

With a binary oppositional perceptual prism for seeing that also values the perspective of the dominant class, it is virtually impossible to grasp the theological significance of God's revelation with regard to issues surrounding the struggle for racial justice. This being case, it is no wonder that good white Christians are rendered virtually silent behind stained-glass windows, trapped as they are in binary oppositional notions of God's revelation that do not allow them to voice real solidarity with the concerns of Black people in the quest for Black lives to matter. Before examining this further, it is important to keep in mind two underlying assumptions.

First, as pointed out in the previous chapter, the white gaze is the prevailing gaze of a nation defined by a white supremacist foundation and ideology. This gaze shapes the collective perceptual cognition of society. Thus, one does not have to be white to be impacted by the white gaze. Nevertheless, as indicated throughout this book, white people are not only most susceptible to having this gaze, but also unlikely to recognize its limitations and interrogate it, for it confirms their experience and vantage point. Put simply, it does not create a natural dissonance for white people as it does for people of color.

Second, and perhaps most important to bear in mind as we move forward, is the fact that, although the silence of good white Christians can be—and usually is—unspoken, it can also be spoken. As we have seen in the clergy "Call for Unity" during the Birmingham protests as well as Bishop Budde's "outrage" regarding Trump, both responses were spoken. Nevertheless, they were expressions of the silence of good white Christians.

What I have come to recognize is that this "silence" often indicates a particular understanding of God's revelation, one shaped by the prism of a white gaze that is blind to the complex feelings of Black people who live with their "backs against the wall" of white supremacy. Consequently, although the silence of good white Christians may take the form of words, it still does not represent genuine solidarity with the struggle against white supremacist affronts to Black life. Even when spoken, it still reads as silence.

God's Love: A Paradox

"Ours is a faith tradition with a crucified Savior at its center. It is time that we take that seriously." This is a refrain I often repeat in gatherings of white church leaders as they wrestle with what this time of racial reckoning means for them, yet just do not seem to get it. During such gatherings, these leaders often express an uncertainty regarding how to really support the Black Lives Matter protests and the impact such protests have on their communities. They admit to being unsettled by the "unrelenting indignation" expressed by the Black protesters. After all, as one faith leader said, "Jesus calls us to love even our enemies. I'm wrestling with what that means in this time." He went on to explain that "God calls us to love everybody," which means, he continued, "that all lives really do matter," yet he did not know how to express this, for he understood the importance of affirming that Black lives mattered. He was in a quandary.

This particular clergyperson was not alone in his dilemma concerning the meaning of God's love when it comes to the Black Lives Matter protests. This has been said to me in varied ways during my numerous conversations with white clergy who have invited me into conversation because they do in fact take seriously their call to racial justice. In other words, these are the good white Christians. What I have come to recognize is that their quandaries are rooted in a white gaze that cannot grasp the paradox that is intrinsic to the very love of God.

The love of God as revealed in Jesus, who is nothing less than the perfect incarnate manifestation of God's love in the world, is a "dynamic transcendent force" that moves through human history. God enters into the "messiness" of human reality to show forth the meaning of God's love. In a sense, this is the paradox of the divine/human encounter itself—it reflects a God entering into solidarity with humanity—taking on the human struggle in all of its complexities in order to show the way toward God's just future, what Jesus called "the Kingdom of God" and Martin Luther King Jr. called the "Beloved Community." This is a way of love. The full measure of God's incarnate love is found in the cross. It is through the cross that the paradoxes which define God's love are definitively disclosed. These are paradoxes that maintain God's utter solidarity with the crucified classes of people. It is these very paradoxes that the binary oppositional white gaze cannot take in—hence the virtual silence of good white Christians when it comes to the complicated issues surrounding the Black struggle.

The issues that have been raised most frequently in my conversations with white faith leaders are forgiveness, violence, and divisiveness. While these are all interrelated and overlapping, I will discuss them separately in an effort to understand the concerns surrounding them and how they relate to the white gaze.

God's Love: A Paradox of Forgiveness

It rarely fails that, when I am speaking with white clergy who are earnestly grappling with racial injustice, they point to the forgiveness displayed in the aftermath of the Mother Emanuel A.M.E. Church slayings as an example of the power of God's love.

Various family members of those murdered in Emanuel Church publicly forgave the white supremacist gunman. In pointing to this act of forgiveness, white clergy with whom I have been in conversation contrast it with the rage and anger often voiced in the protests for Black lives to matter. Essentially, they view the way beyond the protest for racial justice as an either/ or choice between Black forgiveness and Black rage.

In responding, I initially point out that the act of forgiveness, as often displayed in the Black faith tradition, is grounded in the assumption that no human justice can adequately make amends for the grave injustices of white supremacy, including what amounts to a twenty-first-century mass lynching carried out by a white supremacist. Black forgiveness is, first, a sign of faith that God's justice will ultimately prevail. The act of forgiveness serves as a liberating act as it frees those, such as the families of Emanuel, from the anguish of waiting for the proper justice to be enacted. At the same time, Black forgiveness recognizes that the love of God is more powerful than white racist hatred. And so, second, forgiveness frees Black people from being trapped in the cycle of white racist hate, thereby allowing them to appreciate the love of God for them. This is a love that affirms that Black lives do matter. In general, the act of forgiveness frees Black people from the hate of white supremacy that can distort their own sense of self and thus prevent them from moving forward in their own living toward freedom. It is in this way, from the perspective of the victims of hateful injustice, that Thurman suggests we are to hear Jesus's exhortation to love our enemies. "Why such an exhortation?" Thurman asks. Because "once hatred is released, it cannot be confined to the offenders alone."[27] Thus, to forgive is to be freed from a cycle of hate that can become self-destructive.

Now while the focus of forgiveness is not primarily on the perpetrators of white supremacy, the act of forgiveness does provide the perpetrators the opportunity to repent, and thus also to be freed from the cycle of sin in which they are trapped.

---

27. Thurman, *Jesus and the Disinherited*, 86.

With that said, it is equally important to understand that for-giveness is not a palliative for rage/anger. Rather, rage and for-giveness are interrelated.

Black rage is tantamount to prophetic rage, like that ex-pressed by Amos. He railed against the injustice of the Israelites, vehemently proclaiming a time when God's justice would "roll on like a river, righteousness like a never-failing stream." This brings us to the paradox of God's love that is forgiveness. It is a forgiveness that holds the rage. This is most evident on the cross and in the event that was perhaps the final catalyst for Jesus's crucifixion.

Upon entering the temple, at the time of the Feast of the Tabernacles, Jesus threw out those who were buying and selling there. He overturned the tables of the money-changers and then, outraged, proclaimed, "Get these out of here! Stop turning my Father's house into a market-place!" It is telling that in the syn-optic gospels, Mark, Luke, and Matthew, this scene serves as the culminating event leading to Jesus's crucifixion. These gospels overtly link Jesus's rage to the meaning of the cross.

The rage that Jesus feels in this instance, a rage in response to the powerful making use of their privilege, their dominance, to desecrate what is holy, is tantamount to the rage felt by the oppressed when the powerful make use of their privilege, their dominance, to desecrate human beings. Jesus has utter empathy with the feelings of the oppressed, and his solidarity with them will inevitably lead to his crucifixion. Furthermore, it signals the extreme lengths of God's love as a force for justice. In the words of King, Jesus's action in the temple shows that Jesus was "an ex-tremist for love" that will be reified in his crucifixion. It is in this way that the cross once again discloses the paradox that is God's love. It is a love that rages. It is not palliative and comforting. It is unsettling. It is a love that practically necessitates crucifixion. And this brings us back to forgiveness.

Before he breathes his last, Jesus asks God to "Forgive them for they know not what they do." Understood from the vantage point of the One whose very crucifixion signals his solidarity with the rage and struggles of the oppressed, this call for forgiveness is not a milquetoast request. Rather, it is a call for God to release the crucifiers from the cycle of crucifying sin. As such, it serves almost as a harbinger of the resurrection—that is, a call for new life, freed from the crucifying realities of injustice.

In the end, it is only in being able to appreciate the meaning of forgiveness from the vantage point of those who have been harmed by white supremacist hate that the liberating power of God's love for the oppressed can be fully appreciated. Because the white gaze does not allow for a perspective from those on the underside of racial injustice, forgiveness when viewed through the lens of a white gaze is often seen as an antidote to anger/rage. Forgiveness and rage are viewed as oppositional forces. But when it comes to the love of God, they are not. Instead, forgiveness reflects a paradoxical aspect of God's love that is the demand for a change in the way things are—a change from the crucifying realities of white supremacy that precipitate God's rage in the first place.

Before leaving this discussion of forgiveness, there is one more thing that has often struck me in discussions on forgiveness with white faith leaders. Implied in white people's inability to appreciate Black rage is a fear that the rage is a personal attack upon them, an attack that accuses them of being racist. Because of this, a conversation on Black rage turns to a conversation about forgiveness, as it becomes all about the feelings of white people and their need to be delivered from Black rage. Their focus on forgiveness serves almost as a defensive posture to avoid Black rage. In the process, the good white people make themselves, rather than the systems that privilege whiteness, the focus of attention. Again, Black rage it is not necessarily directed toward white people per se. Instead, it is directed against the constructs of white supremacy that privilege white lives and decimate Black lives. Inasmuch as there is Black rage directed toward good white Christians, it is because of their lack of rage regarding white supremacist attacks on Black lives. It is the implied rage behind my son's question, "Where have they been?" And so it is that Black rage, even when directed to good white Christians, is less of an attack and more of an invitation to take up the work needed for liberating change. It is in this way that Black forgiveness contains Black rage, as it too serves as an invitation for good white Christians to repent of their complicity in the very realities that stir the rage. This is the forgiveness that comes from the cross.

Now let's consider another paradox of God's love exposed in the cross—the "nonviolent violence" paradox.

God's Love A Paradox of Violence

After she saw the video of George Floyd's murder, one of my good white Christian friends called to let me know she was offering prayers in "solidarity" with the Black community. I had no doubt that her sentiments and prayers were genuine. Yet I had grown impatient with the earnest prayers of white Christians as they stood quietly on the sidelines while Black lives, especially the lives of Black children, continued to be threatened. So I thanked her for her prayers, but I also reminded her that while prayer was essential, it was not enough. Rather, prayer was just one aspect of what was needed if Black lives were ever to matter. I repeated to her another refrain I have often found myself saying to good white Christians during this time of racial reckoning: "Jesus was not crucified because he prayed too much. Perhaps because he prayed, he was able to go to the cross, but it was not praying that got him crucified."

Jesus was nailed to the cross because he protested the oppressive political, social, cultural, and religious systems and structures of his day, even as he bore witness to God's promised just future. That he was crucified indicates the threatening nature of his protests in regard to the arbiters of oppressive power—hence their attempt to rid themselves of him. That he did not resist his crucifixion reveals his solidarity with the subjugated, dominated, marginalized classes of people of his day in their struggle for life and freedom. The crucifying realities that they could not avoid in their daily lives Jesus did not avoid when it came to his crucifying conviction. It is in this way that Jesus's crucifixion was nothing less than an inevitable consequence for One who in his first public sermon announced that he had come "to proclaim good news to the poor... freedom for the prisoners and recovery of sight for the blind, to set the oppressed free, to proclaim the year of the Lord's favor." Jesus's crucifixion revealed his opposition to the violence of the oppressive realities that threatened the life of the "disinherited" in his world and stood in the way of a more just future. This brings us to the "nonviolent violence" that is God's love, which is perhaps impossible for a white gaze fully to apprehend.

The love that is God's presence is neither passive nor tepid when it comes to injustice. As revealed in Jesus, it is confrontational and passionate. Throughout his ministry Jesus confronted and called out the "demons" of persecuting power. Jesus affirmed the sacred dignity of the "lowly" as he disavowed the rule of the "powerful." He upended the status quo. In so doing, Jesus revealed God's love as a dynamic movement in history that confronts the forces of unjust power. However, systems and structures of unjust power rarely—if at all—surrender quietly. Consequently, the violence that is intrinsic to injustice itself was unleashed, culminating in Jesus's crucifixion.

At this point, it is important to reiterate that injustice in any form is inherently violent and thus to challenge it is to invariably unleash that very violence. Hence, Jesus's protest against the injustice of his day, even though nonviolent in nature, necessarily precipitated a violent response. And it is here that good white Christians can become stymied by a white gaze that cannot hold the paradox of violence that is God's love.

For, inasmuch as they are committed to an understanding of God's love as a nonviolent dynamic that does not countenance violence, it is practically impossible for them to participate in a movement that has the potential to unleash violence. It is made even more impossible by the fact that such an understanding does not readily open one to the perspective of those who have experienced the ever-present violence of injustice—in this instance, the perspective of Black people who have lived with the daily violence of white supremacy, an experience that has the potential to erupt in violent rage. It is this paradox of Black violence that Martin Luther King Jr. addressed as he reaffirmed his commitment to nonviolence, condemning both the "conditions" that created protest as well as the riots, while also recognizing that "a riot is the language of the unheard." Again, this is the paradox that a white gaze cannot contain. Ironically, it is the violence indeed precipitated by the silence, even of good white clergy, regarding the co-morbidities of white supremacy that ravished Black lives long before COVID broke out. King, again, spoke to this type of silence as he admonished the clergy who deplored the violence precipitated by his Birmingham demonstrations yet remained silent regarding the violence suffered by the Black community. He wrote, "I am sorry that your statement did not express a similar concern for the conditions that brought the demonstrations into being."

Essentially, a gaze that is defined by an oppositional binary cannot apprehend the paradox of the "nonviolent violence" of God's love. Given the violent nature of injustice itself, the showing forth of God's love is not an either/or between violence and nonviolence. The love of God that is justice inevitably unleashes the violence of injustice, be it in response to protest or the rage of protest. There is simply no way around the "nonviolent violence" paradox if indeed one is to ever enjoy the more just future that God promises us all.

It was an inability to appreciate this aspect of God's love that led the white clergy in their "call for unity" to practically accuse King of betraying his faith. They admonished him, saying, "hatred and violence have no sanction in our religious and political traditions." In response, King pointed them to the cross. He said, "In your statement you asserted that our actions, even though peaceful, must be condemned because they precipitate violence. But can this assertion be logically made?...Isn't this like condemning Jesus because His unique God-consciousness and never-ceasing devotion to His will precipitated the evil act of crucifixion?"

The crucifixion makes demonstratively clear that a Christian commitment to nonviolence is never simply an either/or choice. To reiterate, if people are committed to contesting the violence that is oppression, then they may have to accept the real possibility of violence that comes with that commitment. But so often they cannot. As one clergyperson said to me, "That's what really turns people off, you know" (meaning white people). And so it was that, even as Bishop Budde proclaimed her solidarity with Black protesters, she made sure to say, "We follow someone who lived a life of *nonviolence* [emphasis mine] and sacrificial love."

The violence that erupts in response to Black protest is the paradox of the cross. This is the paradox of God's love. The inability to fully appreciate that paradox can leave good white Christians trapped in a qualifying silence that bespeaks a white gaze that does not appreciate the violence perpetuated by white supremacy itself. This brings us to a final paradox of God's love discussed here: divisive peace.

The Paradox of Peace

In the midst of the growing racial and political divisions in the nation exacerbated by the MAGA vision, I was scheduled to preach in the Washington National Cathedral on the Sunday when the focus of the gospel reading was Jesus's words, "Do you think that I have come to bring peace to the earth? No, I tell you, but rather division!" Preparing my sermon that week was more of a more daunting task than usual. Playing in my head were the calls for unity, healing, and racial reconciliation that were being voiced, not only by many in the Cathedral community but also by many white faith leaders. Ironically, I found myself in a quandary as to what to preach. What was I to say from the pulpit of the nation's Cathedral about Jesus's proclamation that he came to bring division, not peace? My first thought was, "Really, Jesus? Aren't we divided enough in this country as it is?" But then, I heeded my own words to take the center of our faith seriously — a crucified Christ. In so doing, I recognized the paradox of God's peace. And it was about this paradox that I preached.

In order to fully appreciate the paradox God's peace expressed in Jesus's proclamation about division, one must understand that Jesus's first-century world was no less divided than our nation is today. His was a time of religious, political, and socioeconomic turmoil reflecting the century-long oppressive divides between members of the powerful and wealthy classes versus those who were subjugated and poor. Thus, if there was peace to be found in Jesus's first-century world, it was a peace that masked deep divisions of injustice.

We have here a hint as to why Jesus would want to bring more division to an already divided society.

The division that Jesus brings is the division created by the promised future of God, a future that Jesus so perfectly reveals through both his ministry and person and to which he calls his followers. This is a future that is nothing less than a new order of things. It is a new order in which divisions cease because the peace that is God's justice is made real. As Jesus explained, this is a peace where "the first are last and the last are first," but not because there is an exchange or swapping of positions between the haves and the have-nots, the insiders and the outcasts, the oppressors and the oppressed. Rather, it is because the first are last, the last are first — there is no difference between them, because all are treated and respected as the equal children of God that they are. It is a peace where there are no divisions created by inequity and injustice. Given the state of our world, this means that if Christians are indeed committed to fostering the future that God promises, and hence to following Jesus—then there must be divisions. These are the divisions between the ways of the unjust present and those of God's just future—the divisions that signal the coming of that very just future.

Jesus's mission was not about wreaking havoc. It was about valuing the just peace of God's future as opposed to the "peace" that maintains the unjust status quo. Thus, Jesus disrupted the peace of the time. The justice that he embodied was not without conflict and divisions—as signified again in the cross.

King explained it this way in response to a "white citizen" of Montgomery who confronted him, saying, "Over the years we have had such peaceful and harmonious relations here. Why have you and your associates come to destroy this long tradition?" King responded:

"True peace is not merely the absence of tension; it is the presence of justice.... This is what Jesus meant when he said, 'I have not come to bring peace but a sword....' He seems to have been saying in substance: I have not come to bring the old negative peace with its deadening passivity. I have come to lash out against such a peace. Wherever I come a conflict is precipitated between the old and the new. Wherever I come a division sets in between justice and injustice. I have come to bring a positive peace which is the presence of justice, love, yea even the Kingdom of God."[28]

What King was making clear was what the cross indicates: God's peace, which is justice, disrupts the peace that harbors injustice. In so doing, it lays bare the already existing divides of injustice masked by a "negative peace." This is the paradox of God's love—it is a peace that divides, even as it exposes the divisions of injustice.

---

28. Martin Luther King Jr., *Strive toward Freedom: The Montgomery Story* (1958; Boston: Beacon Press, 2010), 266ff.

In a time of racial reckoning, the peace that is God's love demands a wrecking of the forces of injustice. God's peace, therefore, is not in the first instance harmonious and free of tension, even chaos. It is disruptive and divisive. It is a peace that disrupts white supremacy, exposing the injustice that masquerades as peace as it pushes the nation to live into the vision of its better angels—a vision in which there is justice and freedom for all. Again, this is the paradox that is God's peace. As such, it is a peace that eludes a binary oppositional gaze that sees peace and disruption as antagonistic forces, and thus attempts to avoid the divisions that are necessary for the peace that is justice. Recognizing this helped me gain insight into the long silence of the good white Christians of the Washington National Cathedral community in relation to the Lee/Jackson Confederate windows.

The Cathedral community was avoiding the "disruption" and divisions within the community that they knew removing the windows would create. Consequently, they settled for a "peace" that privileged harmony, even in the case of preserving windows that many recognized as legitimating white supremacist ideology. Community members were essentially trapped in a white gaze that did not allow them to appreciate the paradox of God's peace that leads to a reconciling justice. This was further confirmed for me after a task force was set up to decide what to do about the windows. I was a member of this task force. During our discussions, concerns for the division and disruption that removing the windows would create were repeatedly voiced. In fact, as it became apparent that the windows were likely to be removed, divides within the congregation did emerge—and some people felt so strongly about keeping the windows that they left the Cathedral worshiping community.

Interestingly, it was as a result of hearing the way in which Black people viewed the windows as an affirmation of an ideology that denied their sacred humanity that the decision was finally made to remove them. In opening themselves to the perspective of those whom the white gaze precludes, the good white Christians of the Cathedral were able to transcend that gaze, appreciate the paradox that God's just peace is disruptive, and thus decide to remove the windows.

The point of the matter is that the division into which Jesus calls us is a division that leads to justice. It is a division created when we separate ourselves from a culture of white supremacy that suggests that there are persons more valuable or less valuable than others and then are free to live into a future where all are valued as the sacred children of God that they are. To reach that future requires more than the kind of peace that avoids conflict and promotes harmony. Such peace serves only to mask the divides of injustice. This is, as King says, a negative peace. Such a peace is antithetical to the love of God that moves toward the peace that is justice.

In the end, the way to a future where divisions cease is to strive not for "peace" but for justice. True peace follows justice, not the other way around. The justice that reflects the love of God goes through the cross, which signifies a peace that is divisive.

The White Gaze and the Moral Imagination

Why can't they see? This was a question I asked myself in regard to the Confederate windows in the Cathedral. I wondered why they could not see how hurtful these windows were to Black people. Even while understanding their concern for protecting the "harmony" of the community, I wondered why they could not see how the presence of the windows had already created discord among a significant portion of God's church, namely the Black people who felt divided from a community that provided sacred legitimation to symbols of white supremacy. Why could they not see that their silence perpetuated the harm of white supremacy and not the love of God?

This was the same question I asked when good white Christians, during those twelve days in June when Trayvon's murderer was exonerated and the Voting Rights Act was eviscerated, were virtually silent. Why could they not see that this was an affront to the very love of God that demanded they speak out? Indeed, when I put this question to an eminent white faith leader, he conceded that he did not realize these rulings had struck such a chord within the Black community. I found his response stunning, given that he was one of the good white Christians who was engaged in social justice issues. But later, the shock was mitigated as I came to recognize the impact of a white gaze even on the vision of "good" white Christians.

Why could they not see? It was because of the white gaze. As we have noted, this is a gaze defined by an oppositional binary that not only values the dominant cultural perspective but cannot apprehend paradoxical realities, even the paradox that is God's love. This results in an understanding of God's love that lends itself to virtual silence when confronted by the complicated issues involved in the struggle for Black lives to matter. Such an understanding compromises not only the solidarity of good white Christians with the Black community but also their moral imaginary.

In his "Letter from a Birmingham Jail," King lamented the white church's lack of moral leadership when it came to racial justice. He recalled "a time when the church was very powerful —in the period when the early Christians rejoiced at being deemed worthy to suffer for what they believed. In those days," he continued, "the church was not merely a thermometer that recorded the ideas and principles of popular opinion; it was a thermostat that transformed the mores of society." This was, he said, because of their commitment of those Christians to "a colony of heaven," calling them "to obey God rather than man."[29] In other words, King recalled a time when the Christian

---

29. King, "Letter from a Birmingham Jail."

moral imaginary was not shaped by the prevailing gaze of the society but rather by the love of God. Inasmuch as a white gaze has consciously or unconsciously shaped the perceptions of even the "good" white people, then that time in the church will remain a thing of the past, for the moral imaginary will be constrained by an oppositional binary gaze that cannot embrace the way of God's love that gets us to a future where Black lives will matter. And so where does that leave us?

Back to the Question

"Why didn't they [white clergy] defend Black people from him [Trump]?" my son asked.

My immediate, almost reflexive response was, "Because they are white." I went on to explain to him what a psychologist friend had told me, that "theology can't overcome one's psychology." In answering my son, I meant that being Christian was not enough to overcome what it meant to be white, because it could not overcome the white gaze.

To this, my son responded: "This is what makes me wonder about Christianity because it doesn't seem to be able to make a big difference when it comes to white people being racist. You still got all of these white Christians running around talking about 'Make America Great Again' and nobody saying nothing."

My son's observations echoed those of Niebuhr in his discussion of moral man in immoral society. He said: "The prejudices of honest men are just as great a hazard to ethical relations . . . as the dishonest appeals of demagogues."[30] In terms of "good white Christians," their unwitting support of white supremacist policies though their silences is just as hazardous to the lives of

---

30. Reinhold Niebuhr, *Moral Man and Immoral Society: A Study in Ethics and Politics*, 2nd ed. (Louisville, KY: Westminster John Knox Press, 2013), 136.

Black people and other people of color as is the intentional support that white Christians give to MAGA policies. The impact for all practical purposes is the same: the nation's white supremacist structures and systems are maintained.

W. E. B. Du Bois once observed that if a "nation's religion is its life…white Christianity is a miserable failure."[31] This observation seems prescient. As I came to understand the impact of the white gaze upon even "good" white Christian responses to racial injustice, I found myself wondering with my son about the efficacy of Christianity. I wondered if there was a way to penetrate the white gaze that had seemed to prevent white Christians from grasping the core paradox of Christianity, the crucified savior that is the love of God. Was it possible to free them from this gaze? As I pondered this question, a call from the twenty-seventh presiding bishop of my own Episcopal Church, Michael Curry, took on new meaning for me. It was a call for Episcopalians to join the Jesus movement.

When Bishop Curry first issued this call, many of my non-Episcopal friends asked, "So what were you Episcopalians doing all along?" While this "query" was perhaps meant as more of a rhetorical jest than a serious question, it pointed to a disquieting truth, not simply about the Episcopal Church, but about those "good" white Christians who remained virtually silent as Black lives continued to be claimed by the crucifying realities of white supremacy. For as long as they remained silent, they were not a part of the Jesus movement—a movement through the cross on the way to God's just future. It is in becoming a part of this movement that good white Christians can stand in actual solidarity with Black people in the struggle for our lives to matter. It is in becoming a part of *this* movement that good white Christians can help to upend white supremacy in

---

31. W. E. B. Du Bois, "Of the Culture of White Folk," *The Journal of Race Development* 7, no. 4 (1917), 434–47 at 434, JSTOR, www.jstor.org/stable/29738213.

this nation. Yet it is only in being freed from a white gaze that becoming a part of the Jesus movement becomes possible.

And so, I wondered, what would it require to free good white Christians from a white gaze? What would it look like, I wondered, for good white Christians to join the Jesus movement in a time of heightened racial reckoning? What difference would it make in their responses to complicating matters of racial justice? Would the answer to this question address my son's doubts regarding the efficacy of Christianity in the fight for Black lives, or, for that matter, my own? I was not sure. So I decided to pursue the question.

PART TWO

FROM CRUCIFYING DEATH TO RESURRECTION HOPE

My great-grandparents were born into slavery; they never got to vote. My grandparents voted, but they didn't have that opportunity for much of their lifetime, given the Jim Crow laws that prevented Black people from going to the polls. I always remember my parents voting. In fact, they instilled the importance of voting into my siblings and me. "You must vote for those Black people who never lived long enough to be able to vote," they would say.

My parents did not live long enough to be able to vote for a Black president. And so, when I went to the polls on November 4, 2008, to vote for Barack Obama, I wore a sweater of my mother's along with my father's WWII Marine identification tags around my neck. I wanted my parents to be with me as I voted for the first Black president. They, as well as my great-grandparents and grandparents, could not have imagined such a possibility in a country that for so long deprived Black people of the right to vote. I was voting for at least three generations of my family that day.

And then there was November 3, 2020. Voting on that day was a surreal experience. I was struck by the fact that in my lifetime I was able to vote for the first Black president, Barack Obama, and now I was casting my vote for the first Black female (of South Asian and Jamaican descent) vice president, Kamala Harris. When I went into the voting booth, I literally had tears in my eyes as I thought of my great-grandparents, my grandparents, and my parents. It would have been beyond their wildest imaginings that two Black people could ever be elected to the highest offices in a nation with a Constitution that once declared Black people three-fifths human. I was having trouble believing it myself, even as I cast my vote. Making it even more unbelievable was the fact that we were in the middle of two unrelenting pandemics that were ravaging Black lives—COVID-19 and white supremacy. And so, when I went to the polling place on that November 3, I wore a cap with the words "Black Lives Matter" embroidered across the front. These two voting experiences stand out to me for many reasons, not the least of which is the truth they tell about our country.

As we have seen, on the one hand this nation's very founding identity was defined by a white supremacist ideology. The Constitution that the Framers put in place was based on a "racial contract" in which, as the Dred Scott decision made clear, Black people were granted no rights that white people had to respect. Yet, on the other hand, the founding fathers gave birth to a vision, fleeting as it may have been, of a nation where all persons would enjoy "the unalienable rights of life, liberty and the pursuit of happiness." At the moment of its founding this nation was undecided with regard to what kind of a democracy it wanted to be. And, to this day, it remains undecided. It is, as Part 1 of this book has made clear, a nation fundamentally at war with itself. Throughout our history it has moved back and forth between the two poles of its identity: its "raced" foundation and its vision of equality.

However, from Confederate monuments on the public square to the call to "Make America Great Again," with Black lives in daily peril, one thing has become obvious: this nation is held captive to a moral imaginary defined by whiteness. It is an imaginary that cannot sustain a vision of a society where there is indeed equal justice for all. And to be sure, until it can see its way beyond such an imaginary, there will never be a time when Black lives will really matter. This is where the voices and leadership of white clergy become particularly important.

As faith leaders, clergy are to be accountable to God's vision of a just future. It is a future in which all persons are to be respected as the sacred creations they are. By embracing such a vision and holding the people and leaders of this nation accountable to it, in word and in deed, faith leaders can chart the course for liberating the nation's moral imaginary from the sin of whiteness. Doing so would be the first step in moving the nation to re-imagine itself as a land where, as Martin Luther King Jr. dreamed, people would not be judged by "the color of their skin, but by the content of their character." This would not be a colorblind society, but instead one in which a particular skin color did not automatically bring unfair privilege or undue penalty. Again, this requires a moral imaginary defined by God's vision and not by a white way of knowing the world. While faith leaders in general have responsibility for transforming the nation's moral imaginary, white clergy have a unique role to play.

In a nation where white knowing is privileged and Black knowing is negated, it is white faith leaders who have the social-cultural epistemological privilege and responsibility to challenge the authority of "white knowing" and thus to open up the space for other voices, other experiences, others' knowledge to be heard. If it has shown us nothing else, the attempted overthrow of the nation's democracy by mostly white insurrectionists revealed that those raced white have the "white-skin" privilege that permits them to act boldly in the public square without fear of deadly reprisal. Understanding this means recognizing the power that accompanies that privilege. While it is a power that obviously has destructive potential, it can also have transformative possibilities, particularly when it is exercised by those who are white *and* Christian.

Yet, as we have seen, white Christians have themselves been held captive to the moral imaginary of a white supremacist nation. And so, instead of boldly embracing a "higher moral law" that reflects God's vision for a just future, they have tacitly supported white supremacist actions and fostered anti-Black racism. Where, then, are we to go from here as a nation if even white faith leaders are tethered to a white moral imaginary? From where will come the hope that this nation will ever be able to heed the counsel of its "better angels"?

It is here that Bishop Curry's call for Episcopalians to join the Jesus movement becomes instructive, for this is a movement from the crucifying realities of the cross to resurrection hope for new life. It is only when faith leaders, especially white faith leaders, join this movement that they can become free from a white way of knowing and become the "thermostats" that set the standards for justice and transform the nation's moral imaginary.

In Part 2 of this book, I will look at the significance of a movement from crucifying realities to resurrection hope for people of faith, especially for the white church. We will discuss where the movement from cross to resurrection is calling us in this time of racial reckoning. And we will seek an answer to this question in light of the renewed call for reparations and the global eruption of protest to George Floyd's murder.

4

Resurrecting Reparations

"I can't imagine any reason that I would ever call the police."

This is a pronouncement that my son often makes. In this particular instance, he said it in response to the slaying of Breonna Taylor in her own home in Louisville. Initially, whenever he made this comment, I tried to convince him that there could be an occasion where he might need to call the police. But with every passing incident in which innocent Black lives were lost because someone called the police, I became increasingly aware that my son was right. This awareness grew after the police, called to investigate an alleged domestic issue, shot Jacob Blake seven times in his back, in front of his children. After seeing the video, my son texted, "See what I mean—Black people don't need to be calling the police." I responded, "Yep, best to avoid the police at any cost." I finally became convinced of this after witnessing the police response to the white insurrection at the Capitol.

We cannot be reminded enough that police responded to these protesters with virtually kid gloves. Of course, the police were overpowered by an angry and violent mob of thousands. They were trying to figure out the best way to save their own lives as well as those of congressional leaders. Nevertheless, after that incident I spent many sleepless nights imagining what the scene would have been like if that mob had been Black. For

141

days after, I continued to receive texts from my family and friends decrying with somber awareness that "Black people don't have 'white-skin privilege' in this country," and "It would have been a blood bath on the steps of the Capitol if those insurrectionists had been Black."

My son texted me a comment that was making its way around Black text threads. It read: "We aren't asking you to shoot them like you shoot us. We are just asking you to not shoot us, like you don't shoot them." My son accompanied this with his own comment, "They are not going to shoot people who look like them, but they are going to keep shooting us because we don't."

What I came to realize after the Capitol Hill insurrection was that if Black people, including my son, were ever to feel really safe from police in particular and in this nation in general, there would have to be the kind of reparations that can overcome the notion of white skin privilege and Black skin death that is ingrained in the fabric and collective identity of the nation. Privilege and death, fostered by the white social-cultural epistemology of privilege and the anti-Black narrative, have corrupted the moral imaginary of this nation. And so, I realized that the only way forward was with what I had come to recognize as resurrecting reparations.

Resurrection Reparations

The idea of reparations was brought back to public attention in 2014 when, in his "Case for Reparations," Ta-Nehisi Coates made clear that until the nation reckons with its "compounding moral debts America will never be whole."[1] Coates's call reinforced a resolution (HR-40) that Detroit congressman John

---

1. Ta-Nehisi Coates, "The Case for Reparations," *The Atlantic*, June 2014, https://www.theatlantic.com/magazine/archive/2014/06/the-case-for-reparations/361631/.

Conyers put before the House of Representatives every year from 1989 to 2017, simply asking Congress to establish a commission "to study and consider a national apology and proposal for reparations for the institution of slavery."[2] Texas Congresswoman Sheila Lee Jackson reintroduced the resolution in 2019 after Congressman Conyers's death.

More than half a century ago, at a meeting in Detroit, the National Black Economic Conference issued the "Black Manifesto" demanding reparations. In this manifesto the white religious community was specifically addressed. They were called out for complicity in Black oppression and thus charged with a special responsibility in paying reparations. The manifesto opened by declaring that "racist white America" had exploited the resources, minds, bodies, and labor of Black people. It went on to demand that "white Churches and Jewish synagogues" lead the way by paying $500 million dollars for reparations, because they had "aided and abetted" the "exploitation of colored people around the world."[3] This money was to be used for a range of programs to support economic growth, educational opportunities, and the psychological well-being of the Black community.

On May 4, 1969, James Forman disrupted the services of New York City's Riverside Church, a bastion of white Protestantism, to deliver the manifesto. It was also delivered on that same day at the First United Presbyterian Church of San Francisco and later published in the July issue of the *New York Review of Books*.[4] While some white and Jewish faith communities, as well as seminaries, responded by giving funds to various projects and

---

2. H.R. 40—Commission to Study and Develop Reparation Proposals for African-Americans Act, 115th Congress (2017–2018), https://www.congress.gov/bill/115th-congress/house-bill/40/text.

3. "Black Manifesto," The National Black Economic Conference, July 10, 1969, https://www.nybooks.com/articles/1969/07/10/black-manifesto/.

4. "Black Manifesto."

organizations within the Black community, the goals of the "Black Manifesto" were never achieved.

Nikole Hannah-Jones, the Pulitzer Prize-winning creator of The 1619 Project, has put forth the most recent public call for reparations. "If true justice and equality are ever to be achieved in the United States," she says, "then the country must take seriously what it owes Black Americans."[5] She goes on to argue that, "While unchecked discrimination still plays a significant role in shunting opportunities for Black Americans, it is white Americans' centuries-long economic head start that most effectively maintains racial caste today."[6] Hannah-Jones details the ways in which, starting with slavery, white Americans have been able to accumulate wealth, oftentimes through the labor of Black people, that has provided them with advantages in almost every sector of life. Research from the Brookings Institute concurs with her assessment, noting that "Gaps in wealth between Black and white households reveal the effects of accumulated inequality and discrimination, as well as differences in power and opportunity that can be traced back to this nation's inception."[7]

Over time the Black-white wealth gap has continued to grow, placing Black Americans at an increasing disadvantage with limited opportunities to thrive. For instance, Hannah-Jones says, "You do not have to have laws forcing segregated housing and schools if white Americans, using their generational wealth and higher incomes, can simply buy their way into expensive enclaves with exclusive public schools that are out of the price

---

5. Nikole Hannah-Jones, "What Is Owed," *New York Times*, June 30, 2020, https://www.nytimes.com/interactive/2020/06/24/magazine/reparations-slavery.html.

6. Hannah-Jones, "What Is Owed."

7. Kriston McIntosh, Emily Moss, Ryan Nunn, and Jay Shambaugh, "Examining the Black-White Wealth Gap," Brookings, February 27, 2020, https://www.brookings.edu/blog/up-front/2020/02/27/examining-the-black-white-wealth-gap/.

range of most black Americans."[8] It is for this reason that Hannah-Jones and others argue that reparations must be paid to Black Americans as a first step in addressing the wealth gap, and thus a first step toward repairing the breach created by centuries of white supremacist/anti-Black injustice in our country. Otherwise, maintaining the Black/white wealth gap will signal a society that has no intention of fostering racial justice. As the Brookings report makes clear, "The Black-white wealth gap reflects a society that has not and does not afford equality of opportunity to all its citizens."[9]

As much as the breach of racial injustice is about a wealth gap, it is about more than that. It reflects a gap of choices. The series of choices available to each generation reflects the choices of the previous generation, even as it shapes the choices of the next. In the case of descendants of the enslaved, their choices are shaped by an enslaved forebear who had limited if any choices at all for making a better life. Thus, even if those enslaved in an earlier generation and each succeeding generation made the best choices available, a racialized "choice" gap would remain. No doubt these limited racialized choices reflect a wealth gap, but they also reflect a combination of other social-cultural factors. In many respects, freedom for any community is determined by the options and choices that lie before that community. To start out enslaved is to start out with a "choice deficit," to say the least. With that legacy of limited choices in mind, Richard Rothstein asks a critical question: "What do we, the American community, owe...future generations, for their loss of opportunity? How might we fulfill this obligation?"[10] To repeat, while racial inequality certainly reflects a wealth gap, it most decidedly signals a

---

8. Hannah-Jones, "What Is Owed."

9. McIntosh, Moss, Nunn, and Shambaugh, "Examining the Black-White Wealth Gap."

10. Richard Rothstein, *The Color of Law* (New York: W. W. Norton and Company, Inc., 2017), 213.

"choice gap" as well. Action needs to be taken to repair the breach created by centuries of white supremacist commitments.

There is no doubt that some form of reparation remedy is in order if racial justice is ever to be achieved in this nation. I agree with Hannah-Jones when she says, "Reparations are a societal obligation in a nation where our Constitution sanctioned slavery, Congress passed laws protecting it, and our federal government initiated, condoned, and practiced legal racial segregation and discrimination against Black Americans until half a century ago."[11] However, in the attempt to repair the harm that has been done, and thus to create a world where all persons have equitable life-enhancing choices, reparations must go beyond compensatory payments and remedies. Rather than simply looking back, reparations must also look forward. Reparations must address the gap between the nation as it is and the nation's vision of itself as a place where all persons have equal opportunities for "life, liberty and the pursuit of happiness." In other words, reparations should also demonstrably chart a comprehensive path to a more just future. Otherwise, they become little more than a salve for white guilt while the nation remains trapped in a white moral imaginary that allows the sin of white supremacy to thrive. In other words, without a form of reparations that gets rid of all that fuels the historically complex layers of white privilege and creates the social, economic, and cultural soil to produce an equitable society, then reparations will be nothing more than a nation's effort to assuage its guilty conscience. In fact, most of the responses to the renewed call for reparations have come in the form of apologies or "restitution" programs, such as scholarships or support of Black institutional initiatives, without any substantive systemic change.

My Episcopal denomination issued such an apology, expressing "profound regret that the Episcopal Church lent the institu-

---

11. Hannah-Jones, "What Is Owed."

tion of slavery its support and justification based on Scripture."[12] Various Episcopal dioceses and seminaries proceeded to issue similar apologies, removing the names of slaveowners from their buildings and initiating restitution programs. For instance, the Diocese of Maryland established a $1 million "seed fund" to benefit the Black community within Baltimore and other areas of the diocese. Maryland's bishop explained what motivated this commitment to reparations: "Why should we continue to benefit as an institution," he said, "when so many in the Black community have never had the opportunity to have a good education, good jobs, or good medical care? We've benefited from racist institutions, and now we are going to invest financially."[13] The New York and Long Island dioceses created similar funds. The Episcopal Virginia Theological Seminary also established a $1.7 million reparation fund to be used to support scholarships and other programs geared toward the Black community.

While these types of funds are important and meaningful to confessing institutional complicity in slavery and its legacy, the legacy continues. The point is that compensatory and restitutional reparations are not aimed at creating a different path forward. Despite such reparations, genuine though they might be, the systems and structures that have created the wealth and choice gaps and the need for reparations in the first place endure even as new policies are put in place to further stifle Black success. And Black people continue to be killed with alarming regularity by police officers. So again, even if one could find a way to compensate for the wealth and choice gaps that the racist past has created, it would still not be enough—especially for faith communities.

---

12. "Prayers, Tears and Song Mark Episcopal Repentance for Slavery," Episcopal News Service, October 3, 2008, https://episcopalchurch.org/library/article/prayers-tears-and-song-mark-episcopal-repentance-slavery.

13. Jonathan Pitts, "Maryland Episcopal Church Commits $1 Million to Reparations Seed Fund," *Washington Post*, September 18, 2020.

Faith communities are as obligated as the nation itself to provide reparations, not simply because of the ways in which they have participated in sustaining racial injustice, but because it is what the justice of God demands. Frederick Douglass alluded to this when he compared God's treatment of the once-enslaved Hebrews to the federal government's treatment of formerly enslaved Black people. He wrote, "When the Hebrews were emancipated, they were told to take spoil from the Egyptians.... But not so when our slaves were emancipated. They were sent away empty-handed, without money, without friends and without a foot of land on which they could live and make a living. Old and young, sick and well, were turned loose to the naked sky, naked to their enemies."[14] And so, again, this obligation should focus on the future.

Inasmuch as faith is about partnering with God to mend an unjust world and thus to move us toward a more just future, then faith communities, by definition, are accountable to that future. Given this defining accountability, faith communities are required not simply to look back but to look ahead. Adapting the words of liberation theologian Gustavo Gutiérrez, the task of faith communities is "to reflect upon a forward-directed action" that does not "concentrate on the past. Rather, [reparations should] penetrate the present reality... driving history toward the future."[15]

Where faith communities are concerned, reparations must not simply respond to the crucifying past that is the sin of white supremacy. To limit one's response in this way is actually to still be held captive to that very sin. It is no wonder, therefore, that while there may be changes enacted, white supremacy is maintained. Thus, faith communities must find ways to become liberated from the sinful past by opening their moral imaginary to

---

14. Quoted in Hannah-Jones, "What Is Owed."

15. Gustavo Gutiérrez, *A Theology of Liberation*, 15th Anniversary Edition (Maryknoll, NY: Orbis Books, 1973, 1988), 11.

the promises of God's future. Essentially, faith communities are called to help the nation re-set its moral imaginary.

This is no doubt easier said than done, and is not an overnight or even one generation's achievement. It is an ongoing process that must begin with a commitment to resurrecting reparations. Resurrecting reparations reflect a commitment to creating ongoing possibilities for Black life, to eradicating the crucifying conditions that have fostered Black death, and to enacting systems and structures that allow Black life to flourish. Such a commitment would serve to repair the gap not only of inequality between the white and Black community but also between the nation's unjust present and God's just future. In essence, resurrecting reparations are focused on fostering new life for a community long trapped in historical contexts of crucifying death.

Practically speaking, what does this mean? It is to this question we will now turn.

Re-Configuring Social Memory

Re-configuring social memory is essential to resurrecting reparations. In this country, social memory is a constructed memory that preserves white social-cultural epistemological privilege. It does so by forging the nation's story in such a way as to legitimate a white way of knowing society and the world. As such, it is the discursive power essential to sustaining white supremacist hegemony. If the nation is to move beyond a white moral imaginary controlling its concept of justice, then its social memory must be re-configured.

We must begin to change the story that is passed down from generation to generation. As long as the story that is passed down centers on a white way of knowing that does not accurately acknowledge the systemic and structural constructs that privilege whiteness, then it becomes impossible to chart a different course for the future. From generation to generation the moral imagination will remain captive to the false narratives of history. The sins of one generation are passed down to the next. As Richard Rothstein puts it, "If young people are not taught an accurate account of how we came to be segregated, their generation will have little chance of doing a better job of desegregating than the previous ones."[16] Thus, resurrecting reparations must begin with "engaging in the kind of historical truth-telling that our nation needs" in order to move forward.[17] This is a truth-telling defined by a particular kind of remembering: "anamnesis."

Anamnesis Remembering

The notion of anamnesis derives from Jesus's command at what has become known as his Last Supper. "*Do this in remembrance of me*," he commanded his disciples. The Greek word for remembrance used in the gospel accounts in this command is *anamnesis*. This word points to more than just a mental recall of events. Rather, it is about bringing the past together with the present. Jesus is calling his disciples to bring a memory of him into their present. Furthermore, this is to be an incarnate memory. For, as he lifts up wine and bread, he says, "This is my body.... This is my blood which is given to you.... Do this in remembrance of me." Through this act, Jesus is symbolically connecting his incarnate reality to the call to remember. He is asking the disciples to re-embody him, that is his ministry, in their present. Simply put, Jesus's call is a charge to his disciples to embody in their present their memory of him. Such a remembering would reflect a movement from crucifying realities toward God's promised future. This is the kind of memory to which Jesus is calling all

---

16. Rothstein, *The Color of Law*, 199.

17. Paraphrased from interview with Bryan Stevenson. Transcript: "Race in America: Fighting for Justice with Bryan Stevenson," *Washington Post Live*, October 14, 2020, https://www.washingtonpost.com/washington-post-live/2020/10/14/transcript-race-america-fighting-justice-with-bryan-stevenson/.

those who follow him. It is an "anamnesis remembering" which provides the key to reconfiguring social memory. It does this in several ways.

First, anamnesis remembering involves more than the white community—or even faith leaders for that matter—simply excavating the story of their family's or social and religious institution's historical participation and complicity in Black oppression. While truthfully confronting that past is an important part of "airing of family secrets, [and] settling with old ghosts," anamnesis remembering demands more than this.[18] For this kind of "airing of family secrets" typically engages history from the vantage point of the dominant privileged oppressor class. It is about those who inherited the legacy of slaveholders reckoning with their past, and how that past has shaped their present. Essentially, this kind of truth-telling engages history through a white gaze. Even in retrieving uncomfortable parts of history, it reflects a white telling. It is a white knowing of a white history. In the words of James Baldwin, "The things that most white people imagine that they can salvage from the storm of life is really, in sum, their innocence."[19]

It is no wonder, therefore, that such truth-telling most often leads only to apologies and restitution programs that change nothing. For, regardless of the disreputable family secrets it may unearth, it does not necessarily engage the truth of those who suffered from those long-buried secrets. As well intentioned as it may be, such truth-telling does not reflect a new epistemology of knowing, and thus does not compel a radical re-thinking of the historical present, without which a new moral imaginary remains impossible.

Anamnesis remembering changes the gaze through which history is viewed. The remembering to which Jesus calls his

---

18. Coates, "Case for Reparations."

19. James Baldwin, "The Black Boy Looks at the White Boy," in *Nobody Knows My Name*, International Edition (New York: Vintage, 1961, 1993), 217.

followers, inasmuch as it is to embody his ministry, must begin from the perspective of the crucified, for it was into crucifying conditions that Jesus entered history, as indicated by his manger birth. James Cone put it this way as he compared Jesus's manger birth to the crucifying realities in which Black people have been historically trapped: "He was born in a stable and cradled in a manger (the equivalent of a beer case in a ghetto alley)." Regardless of the historical validity of this story, Cone goes on to explain, theologically speaking, Jesus's manger birth story reflects "the early Christian community's *historical* knowledge of Jesus as a man who defined the meaning of his existence as being one with the poor and outcasts."[20] The Black enslaved testified to this in song: "Poor little Jesus boy / Born in a manger / World treat him so mean / Treat me mean too."

Furthermore, as mentioned in the previous chapter, Jesus made his ministerial "gaze" and priority clear in his first public proclamation, when he said:

> The Spirit of the Lord is on me,
> because he has anointed me
> to proclaim good news to the poor.
> He has sent me to proclaim freedom for the prisoners
> and recovery of sight for the blind,
> to set the oppressed free,
> to proclaim the year of the Lord's favor.

In the words of Howard Thurman, Jesus's ministry was defined by the experiences of the "disinherited," those "who stand with their backs against the wall."[21] Essentially, the vision of God's future about which Jesus preached and his ministry was directed was defined by bringing the new life of justice to

---

20. James H. Cone, *A Black Theology of Liberation*, Fiftieth Anniversary Edition (Maryknoll, NY: Orbis Books, 2020), 120–21.

21. Thurman, *Jesus and the Disinherited*, 7.

the "oppressed" of his day. Thus, the anamnesis remembering that resurrection reparations demand is one that engages history from the vantage point of those on the underside of white supremacy—the enslaved, the lynched, those whom Jim Crow sought to terrorize and destroy.

Anamnesis remembering must resurrect the subjugated knowledge of the Black oppressed. The knowledge they have imparted through narratives, testimony, song, prayers, poetry, and other artifacts of knowing needs to provide the prism, the very starting point, through which history is to be interrogated. It is this historical memory that is to be brought forward into the present to uncover the complexities of white supremacy that have in fact created the gaps of racial injustice, and most significantly the gap between the present and God's future.

There are two a priori assumptions that inform the significance of anamnesis remembering. First, if we are serious about creating a more just society, then we must get to the root of the injustice itself. Honestly confronting and grappling with the nation's difficult and even disreputable past is essential if we are to understand the "problem of the color-line" that threatens to tear the nation apart, even before it bursts forth onto the public square in protest. Doing this means, in the words of James Baldwin, determining the "price of the ticket" the nation has paid to sustain its white supremacist foundation. No one has paid a greater price than those who have been gravely penalized for not being white. While the price for white people may mean wrestling with the ill-gotten gains of white privilege, the price for those not raced white has been limited life choices and thus being unduly trapped in conditions that foster death.

Until we address the price that people of color—especially the least of them—have paid, then racial justice in this nation will be forever elusive. There is no easy way around it; anamnesis remembering must begin with those whom Missouri Congresswoman Cori Bush describes as "the counted outs, the forgotten abouts, the marginalized, and the pushed asides,"[22] those, she says, "who have the least, who've suffered the most."[23] In a society defined by white supremacy, these are disproportionately Black people. Again, Jesus makes clear that the people who reflect the preferential vantage of anamnesis remembering are society's "least of these." In his words: "Truly I tell you, just as you did it to one of the least of these who are members of my family, you did it to me."

The point is that it is only when those who have been on the underside of justice begin to experience justice that we will know we are on the way to the just future that God promises. As theologian Vincent Lloyd rightly notes, "Those who face the full force of domination every day have particular expertise on domination. Those who are less severely affected by domination tend to be enraptured by the will to dominate, with its pretensions to innocence. . . . Those who have the most reason to doubt the wisdom of the world . . . ought to serve as guides to Christian thought and practice."[24]

In the words of Jesus, it is when the oppressed are set free from being captive to injustice that the just future that is God's heaven will come to earth. The U.S. Conference of Catholic Bishops put it this way: "The extent of their suffering is a measure of how far we are from being a true community of persons," that

---

22. Jared Leone, "Missouri Voters Elect Cori Bush, First Black Woman to Congress," kkvx.com, November 4, 2020, https://www.kkyx.com/news/trending/missouri-voters-elect-cori-bush-first-black-woman-congress/5CDFGPNOT 5B2ZOGVC7 GFULX5GQ/.

23. Cori Bush, "Congresswoman-Elect Cori Bush: We Organized for Michael Brown Jr., All of Us Are Headed to Congress," *Essence*, November 4, 2020, https://www.essence.com/news/politics/cori-bush-st-louis-congress-movement/.

24. Vincent Lloyd, "Human Dignity Is Black Dignity," *Church Life Journal*, June 16, 2020, https://churchlifejournal.nd.edu/articles/human-dignity-is-black-dignity.

God calls us to.[25] It is for this reason that in a white supremacist society the historical experiences of Black people must provide the preferential gaze through which history is viewed. Black people's stories lay bare the profound and complex realities of injustice that need to be addressed if justice is to be enacted. To reiterate, therefore, resurrecting reparations must start with anamnesis remembering, telling the truth about white supremacy from the standpoint of those who have been on the underside of it. In this instance, it means bringing Black knowing to the normative center of the nation's story. This brings us to the second a-priori assumption.

In engaging the story from the underside of this country's white supremacist history, one thing becomes extraordinarily clear: it is not simply a story of people being acted upon; they acted back. Oftentimes when history is engaged through the prism of those in power, it fails to recognize the agency of the oppressed themselves. This is one of the ways in which social-cultural epistemological privilege works to support power. As we have seen, this kind of privilege distorts history so that it appears that the way things are is an inevitable historical development. In this instance, it presents Black people as compliant participants in their own oppression, such as happy, docile slaves—or at least, as not being active participants in the struggle for their freedom. Engaging history from a Black perspective reveals that Black people were not compliant participants in their own oppression and were in fact active agents in the fight for their freedom. Most significantly, as they fought for their freedom, they kept alive the vision of the nation's better angels, of a place where all people could live free.

It is within the history of the Black American struggle that the vision of a democracy defined by equal justice is most vibrant.

---

25. United States Conference of Catholic Bishops, *Economic Justice for All: Pastoral Letter on Catholic Social Teaching and the U.S. Economy*, 1986, https://www.usccb.org/upload/economic_justice_for_all.pdf.

This, in and of itself, suggests that if the true story of this nation's democratic project is going to be told, it must begin with those who have been at the center of keeping it alive. With each step Black people have taken toward their freedom, they have actually contributed to the perfection of democracy itself. This is the story that The 1619 Project tells. Words from that project are worth quoting at length:

> But it would be historically inaccurate to reduce the contributions of black people to the vast material wealth created by our bondage. Black Americans have also been, and continue to be, foundational to the idea of American freedom. More than any other group in this country's history, we have served, generation after generation, in an overlooked but vital role: It is we who have been the perfecters of this democracy.
>
> The United States is a nation founded on both an ideal and a lie. Our Declaration of Independence, approved on July 4, 1776, proclaims that "all men are created equal" and "endowed by their Creator with certain unalienable rights" . . .
>
> Yet despite being violently denied the freedom and justice promised to all, black Americans believed fervently in the American creed. Through centuries of black resistance and protest, we have helped the country live up to its founding ideals. And not only for ourselves—black rights struggles paved the way for every other rights struggle, including women's and gay rights, immigrant and disability rights.
>
> Without the idealistic, strenuous and patriotic efforts of black Americans, our democracy today would most likely look very different—it might not be a democracy at all.[26]

---

26. Nikole Hannah-Jones, "The Idea of America," The 1619 Project, *New York Times Magazine* (August 18, 2019), 16, https://www.nytimes.com/interactive/2019/08/14/magazine/black-history-american-democracy.html.

The 1950s and 1960s civil rights struggle reflects the legacy of this 1619 story: "courageous Black people put on their Sunday best and they went to places to push this country to embrace full democracy, to embrace civil rights."[27] And it is the 1619 legacy that was carried forth during the 2020 presidential election when—despite the extraordinary attempts to suppress the Black vote—Black people, especially Black women, came out in record numbers to defeat the white supremacist vision to "Make America Great Again."

The point is that, historically speaking, Black people have not been guided by a white moral imaginary. For such a moral imaginary, as has been pointed out throughout this book, cannot contain a future where Black life is truly free from the crucifying actualities of white supremacy. Consequently, Black people have been able to see beyond the possibilities of a vision that equates white privilege with justice. They have been able to envision a future defined by God's justice, a future in which the sacred humanity of each person is honored and respected. It is this transcendent vision that has inspired Black people's persistent fight for freedom and expanded their imagination of what justice can look like. The enslaved testified to such a vision when they sang,

> I've got shoes, you've got shoes
> All of God's children got shoes
> When I get to Heaven goin' to put on my shoes
> Goin' to walk all over God's Heaven.[28]

On the impact of Black people being guided by the possibilities of God's justice, as opposed to being constrained by a white moral imaginary, James Cone puts it this way: "The idea of

---

27. Transcript: "Race in America: Fighting for Justice with Bryan Stevenson."

28. Negrospirituals.com, https://www.negrospirituals.com/songs/ going_to_ shout_all_over_god_s_heaven.htm.

heaven provided ways for black people to affirm their humanity.
... It enabled blacks to say yes to their right to be free by affirming God's promise to the oppressed of the freedom to be."[29] He
continues by saying that "the image of heaven served function-
ally to liberate the black mind from the existing values of white
society, enabling black slaves to think their own thoughts and
do their own things."[30]

This is the history that anamnesis remembering must fore-
ground. Interestingly, it is in itself a resurrecting story. It is that
story of a crucified people resurrected to fight for the vision of
God's justice. In doing this, they resurrect a nation's vision of justice from the crucifying realities of its white supremacist foundation. The Black struggle for freedom reflects Jesus's movement in
history from crucifying realities to God's promise of new life. It
is in this way that anamnesis remembering, in re-configuring social memory, is essential to resurrecting reparations.

Again, white faith leaders have a significant role to play in
this regard, starting with their own communities and congregations. This was brought home to me when I was asked to help
write a prayer to honor the ratification of the Thirteenth
Amendment. In writing the prayer, my colleagues, good white
Christians all, initially put forward a prayer of thanksgiving
which, with the exception of Frederick Douglass, did not include names of Black abolitionists. While they included names
of white abolitionists who denounced slavery, these abolitionists did not necessarily affirm Black equality. That they did not
include the names of other Black freedom fighters was an example of social memory blotting out these names from their
own memory. It illustrated how white knowing erases Black
history. Even in the names it included, the prayer reflected the
privileged "white knowing" of history. If that prayer had not

29. James H. Cone, *The Spirituals and the Blues: An Interpretation* (Maryknoll, NY: Orbis Books, 1991), 82.

30. Cone, *The Spirituals and the Blues*, 86.

been altered to include Black abolitionists, it would have reinforced that knowing. I changed the prayer.

While the prayer my white colleagues submitted did not reflect an intention to deploy the discourse that sustains white supremacy, their intention did not matter. The result would have been the same. As many times as the prayer would have been prayed (it has since become the official prayer of the diocese and was adopted by other dioceses as well), it would have reinforced the notion of white superiority. The absence of Black people from the fight for freedom, even in this prayerful reflection, unwittingly affirmed the trope of Black people as passive recipients of white ingenuity and largesse. In including the names of white abolitionists who deemed Black people inferior, they at best obscured the sinister realities of white supremacy. While there is no doubt that this prayer exemplified unwitting complicity in promoting a social memory that sustains white supremacy, once its authors were made aware of the problems with it, they would no longer be able to claim ignorance. If indeed, they had unwittingly found themselves complicit in sustaining a white knowing, then they needed to be intentional in fostering a different way of knowing. The first step would be commitment to anamnesis remembering. This would mean first educating themselves on the history of slavery and its legacy through the eyes of the enslaved, which would provide them with the knowledge to write a different kind of prayerful story. Through the prayers that are prayed, the stories that are told, the saints who are celebrated—informed with anamnesis remembering—white faith leaders can significantly help to re-configure social memory and thus help to free white Christians from a white moral imaginary.

In the final analysis, re-configuring social memory is the essential first step to resurrecting reparations, and this begins with anamnesis remembering. Anamnesis remembering releases the secrets of the past, which, in the words of Toni Morrison, have been the "lies" and "evasions" of white knowing, thus opening us to a future beyond the constraints of white imaginings. As she succinctly noted, this is a future that "can be more liberating than any imagined future if you are willing to identify its evasions, its distortions, its lies, and are willing to unleash its secrets."[31]

Resurrecting Re-Imagining

But of course, resurrecting reparations necessarily involve more than re-configuring social memory, of which anamnesis remembering is a part. Given the vitality of an anti-Black narrative that has penetrated the nation's collective consciousness, it also requires a resurrecting re-imagining of the Black body. While centering the Black historical story helps to do this, more is needed to, at the very least, mitigate the anti-Black tropes that incite fatal assaults upon Black bodies. Resurrecting reparations must include sustained efforts to re-imagine the Black body so that it is perceived as human and not beastly. Such re-imagining work begins with proximity. Now, even as I discuss these various aspects of reparation remembering separately, they will, as we shall see, reinforce each other.

Creating Proximity

Howard Thurman reminds us that there is no soil more fertile in which stereotypes and even hate can fester and grow than the soil of separation and division. Where there is isolation from our fellow humans, Thurman says, fear and prejudice take root, fostering hate and stifling empathy. It is for this reason that proximity is important to re-imagining the Black body.

In general, proximity helps transform the collective imagination regarding those who have been socially vilified. It does

---

31. Toni Morrison, Wellesley College Commencement Address, May 28, 2004, https://www.c-span.org/video/?182148-1/wellesley-college-commencement-address.

so by closing the distance between the privileged and those whom the privileged have othered. It brings the othered into their sphere of concern. It helps the privileged to see that those caricatured as not like them are indeed just like them—with bodies that can be hurt and need healing, hearts that can be broken and need love, and souls that can be lost and need salvation.

Jesus reveals the importance of being proximate, or near, in his words to his disciples: "And if you greet *only* your friends, what more are you doing than others?" Essentially, Jesus is calling his disciples to reach beyond their small circle of friends to those who indeed have been othered, those whom the disciples perhaps viewed as outside of their concern. For them to reach beyond their "closed" circle would actually reflect the anamnesis remembering that Jesus calls them to, as it is a reflection of his own ministry. Jesus was intentionally near to the dehumanized and demonized of his day. These were the lepers, the Samaritans, the blind, the widows, the prisoners—these were the Black people of Jesus' time. From touching the leper to going to Samaria and initiating a conversation with a Samaritan woman, Jesus brought those most othered into his circle of care and salvation. In doing this, he contested social, cultural, and even religious narratives of his day that rendered the "othered" undeserving of compassion, blamed them for their suffering, and effectively relegated them to being unworthy of God's justice. There is no doubt that the lack of proximity has aided and abetted attacks on Black bodies and impeded the potential for racial justice in our nation.

Recent studies have revealed the harsh reality that 75 percent of white Americans have "entirely white social networks without any minority presence." Of the 25 percent that are not homogeneous, their social circles are still 91 percent white.[32] It is

---

32. Daniel Cox, Juhem Navarro-Rivera, and Robert P. Jones, "Race, Religion, and Political Affiliation of Americans' Core Social Networks," PRRI, August 3, 2016, https:// www.prri.org/research/poll-race-religion-politics-americans-social-networks/.

no wonder, as we have seen, that Black and white people have widely different views of reality—concerning for instance the impact of systemic racism or of policing in this country. It is also unsurprising that deeply embedded within white collective consciousness there is a fear of Black people as dangerous and violent beasts, ready to explode with little provocation. Hence, as has been shown, simply the appearance of a Black person is enough to justify calling the police. Contributing to this is the fact, that, as Robert Jones points out, most whites are not "socially positioned" to understand Black people's experience, let alone get to know them beyond the tropes that characterize the pervasive anti-Black narrative. Again, racial distance, that is racial segregation, is the social-cultural fuel that feeds and sustains the anti-Black narrative, not to speak of profoundly different perceptions of reality.[33] This is another reason that Hannah-Jones and others have focused on closing the wealth gap as essential to reparations, given the way in which the wealth gap promotes racial segregation in all sectors of life in the nation. But beyond closing the wealth gap there must be other ways to foster proximity. And this is where white faith leaders are essential.

Faith communities are as segregated as society itself. For the most part, Martin Luther King's observation remains true, that "eleven o'clock on Sunday mornings is one of the most segregated hours, if not the most segregated hour in Christian America."[34] While there has been some improvement since the time of his observation more than fifty years ago, "research 'reveals' that 8 in 10 (86%) have congregations with one predominant

---

33. Christopher Ingraham, "Three Quarters of Whites Don't Have Any Non-White Friends," *Washington Post*, August 25, 2014, https://www. washington post.com/news/wonk/wp/2014/08/25/three-quarters-of-whites-dont-have-any-non-white-friends/.

34. See clip from *Meet the Press*, April 29, 2014, https://www.youtube.com/ watch?v=1q881g1L_d8/.

racial group.'"[35] As one religious reporter put it, "Christian America has become ironically inseparable from a theology of division and racial segregation."[36]

White faith leaders, therefore, must be intentionally committed to fostering racial proximity, thus bringing their communities closer to the Black experience. The proximity that resurrecting re-imagining compels involves more than yearly racial justice/civil rights pilgrimages or exchanges with Black congregations. As well intentioned as these types of experiences may be, they tend to objectify Black people as objects to be studied, or as a source of knowledge. They foster what Martin Buber might describe as an I-it relationship, as opposed to an I-Thou relationship. They do not necessarily foster genuine relationships of mutuality and reciprocity. Rather, they sustain an unequal relationship as white people set the grounds for knowing, while Black people fill white people's identified knowledge gap. When I have been involved in these types of encounters, I have often felt like the Black experience is on display as in a zoo, and that I am there to provide the intellectual performance the white visitors demand of me. The point here is that these types of programs entail white people comfortably *passing through* the Black experience in which I live.

The proximity to which Jesus calls his followers requires concerted and sustained encounters with the Black experience that do not objectify Black people. Such encounters help foster a re-imagining of the Black body that will lead to eliciting responses of care and kindness as opposed to outrage and fear when encountering Black people in everyday life. Admittedly,

---

35. Andy Gill, "Is the Most Segregated Hour of Christian America Still Eleven O'Clock on Sunday Morning?" January 17, 2018, https://www.patheos.com/blogs/andygill/segregated-hour-eleven-o-clock-on-sunday-morning/.

36. Gill, "Is the Most Segregated Hour of Christian America Still Eleven O'Clock on Sunday Morning?"

such proximate encounters are not easy to achieve in a society that is comprehensively segregated. Nevertheless, a significant first step would be for white faith leaders to affirm the Black experience as an essential part of the sacred story.

Karl Barth proclaimed that preachers "must hold the Bible in one hand and the newspaper in the other," in order to bring God's revelation into proximity with contemporary concerns. He went on to explain that one should "interpret newspapers from your Bible." These words are instructive for fostering racial proximity. Inasmuch as the newspaper reflects contemporary experiences—which include Black experiences—white faith leaders should be intentional in bringing the realities of day-to-day Black experiences into dialogue with the Bible. Moreover, even as the Bible provides the lens through which to understand that experience, the Black experience also provides the lens through which to interpret the Bible.

When I preach at the Washington National Cathedral, which is a largely white congregation, I often utilize the Black experience to open up the meaning of God's revelation. For instance, on one particular Sunday, when illustrating the meaning of Matthew 25:31–46 that culminates in Jesus proclaiming, "Whatever you did for one of the least of these brothers and sisters of mine, you did for me," I recalled the story of a forty-two-year-old Black woman named Pamela Rush, as highlighted by Catherine Flowers in her book *Waste*.[37] Pamela was a single mother of two children, living in a single-wide trailer in Lowndes County, Alabama. After doing all that she could to improve her family's living conditions and provide life-enhancing opportunities for her children, Pam succumbed to COVID-19, leaving behind two children. In bringing stories like Pam's into conversation with the Bible, several things can occur. It can put a real person with real struggles behind the statistics and stereotypes

---

37. Catherine Coleman Flowers, *Waste: One Woman's Fight against America's Dirty Secret* (New York: The New Press, 2020).

of poor Black people. It can bring the white congregation into proximity with a real, lived Black experience. It can affirm the Black experience as a sacred experience that opens up the meaning of God's revelation. And as it does this, it contests the anti-Black narratives that demonize Black people. Moreover, it does this without objectifying a Black person.

While one story or illustration is not going to automatically transform a collective consciousness so that the Black body is re-imagined, sustained and consistent efforts can. Preaching, without a doubt, provides a powerful and meaningful platform for fostering the proximity essential to a re-imagining of the Black body.

In conjunction with preaching, proximity can be created through other spaces of study and conversation. Projects like The 1619 Project should be essential parts of church curricula. Introducing projects like these into church curricula actually serves to interrupt a white knowing of God while at the same time again affirming the sacredness of the Black experience.

With commitment and a creative imagination, racial proximity can be created within even segregated worship spaces. While this should not be seen as a substitute for genuine interactions with Black people, the fact is that the Black experience can be brought into worship spaces without objectifying Black people, despite there being no Black people present. By doing this consistently, one can lay the foundation for different kinds of responses than those informed by an anti-Black narrative when white people encounter Black people in the public square.

Countering Anti-Blackness

This brings us to another aspect of resurrection re-imagining of the Black body: forthrightly contesting the anti-Black narrative. The anti-Black narrative must be intentionally disrupted and uprooted from white theological consciousness. As pointed out in chapter 1, this narrative has penetrated the Christian theological fabric. Thurman's words provide a vivid description of how this is the case. He says, "God, for all practical purposes, is imaged as an elderly, benign white man, seated on a white throne, with bright white light emanating from his countenance. Angels are blondes and brunettes suspended in the air around his throne to be his messengers and execute his purposes. Satan is viewed as being red with glow of fire. But the imps, the messengers of the devil, are Black."[38]

While not as starkly as in what Thurman describes, the anti-Black theological legacy *is* carried forward in the scriptures, hymns, iconography, and other symbols of Christian churches. As mentioned earlier, it is important to recognize and interrogate the ways in which anti-Black themes remain vibrant within the Sunday-to-Sunday worshiping culture. The ways in which various scriptures promote anti-Black tropes or provide the theological soil for them to grow must not be ignored. They should provide points for discussion. Asking simple questions, like, "What do you think Black people feel when they hear scriptures that equate darkness with evil?" would be a first step in recognizing that such language is not benign. Furthermore, in some instances, traditions of worship may need to be abandoned because of the way in which they promote anti-Blackness. This means certain hymns may simply need to be excluded from the musical canon of worship. In addition, there must be a proactive commitment to include religious iconography that portrays Blackness as sacred. The absence of positive Black imagery is as problematic as the presence of negative Black imagery. Disrupting anti-Blackness means not only interrogating and/or eliminating negative themes, symbols, and imagery having to do with Blackness but also including positive symbols, themes, and imagery. In order to disrupt an anti-Black narrative that cast Black bodies as demonic, there must be images of Black bodies

---

38. Thurman, *Jesus and the Disinherited*, 43.

as reflective of the divine. It is for this reason that images of a Black Christ or a Black Madonna are probably even more significant in white congregations than they are in Black.

While these efforts at re-imaging the Black body may seem trivial, they are important in contesting anti-Black narratives that have been shrewdly deployed by various institutions, including the church. Pro-actively countering this narrative, even in small ways, at every opportunity is one means of intervening in the reflexively hostile white responses to Black bodies.

Even with this, faith leaders must also move beyond their own faith communities and claim their moral voice in the public square. They must lead the way in calling for a national platform for historians, educators, political scientists, writers, and thinkers to guide the nation in reckoning with anti-Blackness and its consequences. It is only when we can confront directly and truthfully the anti-Black narrative that has penetrated the nation's collective consciousness that we will be able to foster a future where Black life will be not just safe, but can thrive.

Let us recap before turning to another significant aspect of resurrecting reparations. What we have seen is that an essential step toward a future free from the sin of white supremacy involves re-configuring social memory, for which anamnesis remembering is significant. Equally important is re-imaging the Black body, to which creating proximity and confronting the anti-Black narrative are essential. What these aspects of resurrecting reparations recognize is that the legacy of white supremacy is not simply manifest in systems, structures, and policies. This legacy is also epistemological and theological. It has forged a pervasive white way of knowing that has been given both subtle and overt theological legitimation. It is this epistemological/theological legacy that constrains the moral imagination, thereby providing the foundation on which white supremacist systems, structures, and policies can be established and thrive with relative impunity. In the end, until the moral imaginary is untethered from a white knowing, America will never be able to live into its own best vision. Bottom-line, without a moral imaginary shaped by a transcendent vision of justice, the breach of white and Black inequality, still less the breach between the unjust present and God's just future, will never be repaired. As a result, Black lives will remain in peril.

Thus, faith leaders who are accountable to God's just future have a primary responsibility to lead the way to a more expansive moral imaginary. They must expand the notion of reparations to be informed not simply by the sins of a crucifying past but by the promise of a resurrecting future. As Vincent Lloyd aptly notes, "It is from the perspective of a redeemed world that we must discern the appropriate protest and policy change."[39] Thus, faith leaders must initiate, beginning within their own communities, a program of resurrecting reparations as an essential component to other reparation programs.

Finally, faith leaders must guard against becoming so "heavenly minded that they are no earthly good," especially with regard to the work of resurrection reparations. In keeping the newspaper in one hand, they must respond to the immediate realities of crucifying death when it comes to Black bodies. Borrowing again from the words of Gutiérrez, we must commit "to action which transforms the present."[40] This brings us to the fatally aggressive policing of Black bodies, which is what keeps me, as well as other parents of Black children, up at night. The fatal policing of Black bodies sends a clear message to the Black community. In the words of Frederick Douglass, "it [is] worth a half-cent to kill a 'nigger,' and a half-cent to bury one," so Black lives don't matter.[41]

---

39. Lloyd, "Human Dignity Is Black Dignity."

40. Gutiérrez, *A Theology of Liberation*, 12.

41. *Narrative of the Life of Frederick Douglass*, in *The Classic Slave Narratives*, edited with an introduction by Henry Louis Gates Jr. (New York: Mentor Books, 1987), 270.

Resurrecting Justice

There has been no cry that has emerged more loudly and created more controversy from the Black Lives Matter movement than the call to "defund the police." This call reflects diverse views regarding reforms that must be enacted to change the ways in which police respond to Black people. While for some defunding the police may mean reallocating funding and for others it may mean some form of abolishing policing altogether, it is ultimately about a community that "wants to see the rotten trees of policing chopped down and fresh roots replanted anew."[42]

What is clear is that one of the most powerful indications that Black lives are worth more than a "half-cent" in this country will be when there is a change in the way police engage with Black bodies. It is worth reiterating that unarmed Black people, most prominently Black males, are disproportionately killed by the police. Black males are 2.5 times more likely to be killed by police than white males.[43] A 2016 *Washington Post* study pointed even more starkly to the deadly impact of policing Black male bodies. It reported that "each month approximately eighteen Black men are killed by law enforcement officers."[44] To list the

---

42. Rashawn Ray, "What Does 'Defund the Police' Mean and Does It Have Merit?" Brookings, June 19, 2020, https://www.brookings.edu/blog/fixgov/2020/06/19/what-does-defund-the-police-mean-and-does-it-have-merit/.

43. Frank Edwards, Hedwig Lee, and Michael Esposito, "Risk of Being Killed by Police Use of Force in the United States by Age, Race, Ethnicity, and Sex," *Proceedings of the National Academy of Sciences* 116, no. 34 (August 2019), 16793–16798; DOI: 10.1073/pnas.1821204116, https://www.pnas.org/content/116/34/16793.

44. Quoted in Katheryn Russell-Brown, "Making Implicit Bias Explicit," in *Policing the Black Man: Arrest, Prosecution, and Imprisonment*, edited and with an introduction by Angela J. Davis (New York: Vintage Books, 2017), 136. For up-to-date data see "Fatal Force," *Washington Post*, https://www.washington post.com/graphics/investigations/police-shootings-database/.

names of unarmed Black persons killed by police would fill a long chapter in this book. Indeed, while writing this very chapter I was interrupted with a text from my sister which read, "Did you hear what just happened here in Columbus? Another Black man killed, for being Black while in his garage." My sister was referring to forty-seven-year-old Andre Maurice Hill.

Police arrived at Andre Hill's house after a neighbor called to report being disturbed by the sound of a car engine going off and on repeatedly. As officers approached Hill, who had a cellphone in his hand as he stood in his open garage, one of the officers fatally shot him. This deadly shooting followed another fatal shooting of a Black man in Columbus two weeks earlier. Twenty-three-year-old Casey Goodson was killed by police as he was returning home from a dental appointment and picking up Subway sandwiches for his family. He was shot in the doorway of his home, where he fell dead with his house key still in the door.

As previously mentioned, studies have shown that the shooting of Black men at such disproportionately alarming rates is about more than "bad policing." Even as it reflects the way in which the anti-Black narrative has insinuated itself into the collective consciousness of society, including that of police officers, it represents the systemic and structural legacy of anti-Black policing in this country. While faith leaders have been reluctant to affirm the chants to "defund" the police, resurrection reparations demand that they become engaged in dismantling the legacy of white supremacist policing, for there is no more crucifying reality than this.

As with resurrection reparations in general, dismantling the legacy of white supremacist policing begins with re-configuring the social memory concerning policing in this country. That means telling the historical truth of policing from the vantage point of those who have been historically on the deadly receiving end of it—Black people. Doing so reveals that anti-Black policing is in the DNA of police ideology and infrastructure. Policing in America emerged as a way to protect white supremacist society—which meant, most notably, patrolling and controlling Black bodies. As researcher Katheryn Russell-Brown points out, "The tensions between African Americans and the police have deep historical roots."[45]

While a comprehensive history of American policing is far beyond the scope of this book, any discussion of changing the way in which police treat Black people must address the fact that patrolling "the comings and goings and movements of Black people" has always been a primary focus of American policing.[46] "Why did American policing get so big, so fast?" asks historian Jill Lepore. "The answer," she says, "mainly, is slavery."[47]

Policing as we know it today, especially in urban areas, emerged with slave patrols. These patrols consisted of both paid and volunteer white people, mostly men between twenty-one and forty-five years of age. The purpose of these patrols was to enforce slave codes like the one Virginia adopted in 1680, which read:

> WHEREAS the frequent meeting of considerable numbers of negroe slaves under pretence of feasts and burialls is judged of dangerous consequence; for prevention whereof for the future, Bee it enacted by the kings most excellent majestie by and with the consent of the generall assembly, and it is hereby enacted by the authority aforesaid, that from and after the publication of this law, it shall not be lawfull for any negroe or other slave to carry or arme himselfe with any club, staffe, gunn, sword or any other weapon of defence or offence, nor to goe or depart from of his masters ground without a certificate from his master, mistris or overseer, and such permission

---

45. Russell-Brown, "Making Implicit Bias Explicit," 139. For up-to-date data see "Fatal Force."

46. Khalil Gibran Muhammad, "American Police," NPR, June 4, 2020, https://www.npr.org/transcripts/869046127.

47. Jill Lepore, "The Invention of the Police," *The New Yorker* (July 13, 2020), https://www.newyorker.com/magazine/2020/07/20/the-invention-of-the-police.

not to be granted but upon perticuler and necessary occasions; and every negroe or slave soe offending not haveing a
certificate as aforesaid shalbe sent to the next constable, who
is hereby enjoyned and required to give the said negroe
twenty lashes on his bare back well layd on, and soe sent
home to his said master, mistris or overseer. And it is further
enacted by the authority aforesaid that if any negroe or other
slave shall presume or lift up his hand in opposition against
any christian, shall for every such offence, upon due proofe
made thereof by the oath of the party before a magistrate,
have and receive thirty lashes on his bare back well laid on.
And it is hereby further enacted by the authority aforesaid
that if any negroe or other slave shall absent himself from his
masters service and lye hid and lurking in obscure places,
comitting injuries to the inhabitants, and shall resist any person or persons that shalby any lawfull authority be imployed
to apprehend and take the said negroe, that then in case of
such resistance, it shalbe lawfull for such person or persons to
kill the said negroe or slave soe lying out and resisting, and
that this law be once every six months published at the re-
spective county courts and parish churches within this
colony.[48]

Slave codes were enacted "to thwart any activity that might
upend the institution of slavery."[49] According to historian Khalil
Gibran Muhammad, these patrols essentially gave white people
"a sense of superiority almost over this whole class of people
that they were now in charge of patrolling."[50]

After Reconstruction the slave patrols evolved to enforce
Black codes. These codes were enacted to keep Black people in

---

48. "Slave Law in Colonial Virginia—A Timeline," https://www.shsu.edu/~
jll004/vabeachcourse_spring09/bacons_rebellion/slavelawincolonialvirginiatime
line.pdf.

49. Russell-Brown, "Making Implicit Bias Explicit," 139.

50. Muhammad, "American Police."

their place, virtually returning them into slavery. As Muhammad explains, "The Black codes, for all intents and purposes, criminalized every form of African American freedom and mobility, political power, economic power, except the one thing it didn't criminalize, the right to work for a white man on a white man's terms."[51] Essentially, the Black codes made "living while Black" a crime.

Modern policing began in 1909 with the appointment of August Vollmer as police chief in Berkeley, California. With him, American policing became more militarized. He proclaimed that policing was about "a war against the enemies of society."[52] Those enemies he designated as "Mobsters, bootleggers, socialist agitators, strikers, union organizers, immigrants, and *Black people*."[53]

What even this brief overview reveals is that the ideology informing the way in which policing was conceived in this country was born out of a commitment to a white supremacist society and was defined by anti-Black tropes that viewed Black people as dangerous beasts. Black people were considered the most threatening "enemies" of white supremacy.

This is the history that must be essentially "resurrected" from the story of policing in America. Only in this way can we re-configure a social memory that has led the white public to deny that racism is a systemic problem in policing. What this history actually reveals is that policing in America functions the way it was initially intended—to control and patrol Black living. It is no wonder, then, that Black people in general, and Black males in particular, are disproportionally accosted and killed by these modern-day slave patrols. White faith leaders must join the call to re-imaging policing in this country. This begins with "defunding" the crucifying apparatus of policing that patrols and destroys Black life, while at the same time supporting the

51. Muhammad, "American Police."

52. Quoted in Lepore, "The Invention of the Police."

53. Lepore, "The Invention of the Police."

establishment of resurrecting systems and structures that protect and foster Black life.

Re-imaging policing requires first and foremost a commitment to establishing just communities. Just communities are
safe communities. They are free from the violence that destroys
Black life. This is the violence of poverty and its crucifying co-
morbidities: indecent housing along with the lack of educational, employment, health care, and recreational opportunities.
It should also be noted that violence breeds violence. The high
rates of homicidal violence in impoverished urban centers are
indicative of the violence that violence creates. In order to stop
the violence that erupts onto the streets, one must stop the violence that is poverty, a social condition in which Black people
are disproportionately trapped. As much research has shown,
"public safety is a product of family and community environments, access to opportunity, educational and health care services, and many other interventions."[54]

Furthermore, to stop this violence and foster just communities, the way in which Black communities are perceived must be
changed so that justice can be enacted. Black communities, like
Black people in general, are viewed through the lens of "retributive justice." Retributive justice begins with the presumption
that sin, in this instance crime, must be punished accordingly.
What we find is that Black people, as well as other poor people,
are actually blamed for the crucifying realities in which they are
trapped. Therefore, instead of being helped to become free from
those realities, they are punished. Harsh policing is a part of that
punishment.

Resurrecting reparations demand a commitment to a resurrecting justice. Such justice creates communities that will foster
life. It names the crucifying conditions in which people are

---

54. Marc Mauer, "The Endurance of Racial Disparity in the Criminal Justice System," in Davis, *Policing the Black Man*, 37.

trapped and works to eliminate them. Resurrecting justice is committed to stopping the violence that destroys life options. Accountable to the more just future that is God's, faith leaders should therefore take the lead in at least calling for a task force of social, political, economic, business, and faith leaders to develop an urgent plan to address and eliminate poverty with all of its social comorbidities in this country. To reiterate, communities that foster life are safe communities; they are communities free of fundamental social violence.

Faith leaders must also lead in articulating the call to defund the police, not as a call to abolish safety, but quite the contrary, as a call to foster resurrecting justice. For as policing functions today, it reflects another aspect of the crucifying violence in which Black lives are trapped. It is for this reason that faith leaders must boldly call for a reallocation of federal, state, and local funding priorities and creative energy toward building just/safe communities as opposed to policing communities. More specifically, a model of resurrecting justice requires shifting from community police to community responders such as social workers, mental health workers, pastors, teachers, and so forth. The fact is that every 911 call does not require a response from law enforcement. Recognizing this would go a long way to preventing the Black deaths at the hands of police responding to calls of concern for a family member in crisis. This is actually the model supported by many who call for "defunding of the police," for they rightly recognize that moving to what many have called "safety responders," as opposed to police, would serve to "decriminalize" many of the crises that typically emerge from a life trapped in crucifying realities. As racial justice advocates have pointed out, "This approach further enhances the push to decriminalize and destigmatize people with mental health conditions and addiction problems."[55] Overall, such a model is compatible with the notion of resurrecting reparations, which seek

---

55. Ray, "What Does Defund the Police Mean?"

to restore life possibilities for those trapped in life-denying realities. And to be sure, a model of community responders would in fact allow for my son to "never have to call the police," yet still call for help if he ever needed it.

In the final analysis, white supremacist/anti-Black violence must be recognized as a national emergency in this nation. From the daily conditions in which Black lives are trapped to police brutality, Black people are disproportionately caught in a crucifying web that portends their death. In order to address it, more than compensatory reparations are required. At a minimum, there must be a comprehensive commitment to resurrection reparations that foster a moral imaginary able to contain a vision that provides opportunities for Black lives to survive and thrive. As this chapter has attempted to show, white faith leaders have a special role to play—because of both their white and Christian identities. This dual identity can serve as an impediment to racial justice or as a help in advancing racial justice. It is left to white faith leaders to determine which it will be. The choice of one will require only silent compliance, while the other will require the bold and hard work of resurrection reparations.

We should note here that a commitment to resurrection reparations actually focuses on the very message and movement of Jesus. It does so with an emphasis on corporate social sin as opposed to individual sin. When talking about racial injustice, therefore, the question is not whether an individual is racist or anti-Black, but how society is held captive to the sin of anti-Black white supremacy. Hence, the atonement that is required concerns repairing the breach between the present world and God's just future as opposed to repairing a breach between an individual and God. Simply put, resurrection reparations are about the sin of the world. And this is what the Jesus movement was all about. But, so what?

Lingering Doubts

"So what?" This is the question my son asked me as we talked about reparations and the call to defund the police. "So what?" he asked. "What difference is all of that really going to make?"

He is never slow to text me each day with the news of police officers being exonerated for killing Black people. "Did you hear the latest?" he texted one morning. "The officer who killed Breonna Taylor is being charged with endangering the people who lived next door because his bullet went into the wall. Didn't matter that he killed her. Guess her life didn't matter."

Later that day, in conversation, he exclaimed, "I really don't know why Black people are so hopeful. Things really are just not going to change."

And so that left me truly wondering: Why are we so hopeful? From whence does our hope come?

5

Resurrection Testimony

"How is the Black Lives Matter protest really making a difference?"

This was the text I received from my son in response to a video of a nine-year-old Black boy being prevented from eating in a restaurant in my son's city of Baltimore. The white manager said the outfit the Black child was wearing violated dress code. Yet, as the mother pointed out, a little white boy was allowed to eat in the restaurant wearing an outfit remarkably similar to the one her Black son was wearing. As the mother later remarked, "I have faced racism time and time again, but it's hard . . . when you have to see your child . . . upset because he knows he's being treated different than a white child!"[1]

As Black Lives Matters protests began to erupt across the nation and the world, the daily assaults on Black lives continued. It also seemed that various "micro-aggressions" targeting Black people were increasing; at least reports of them were. There was the white female restaurateur who called the police on a woman

---

1. Alicia Lee, "A Restaurant Denied Service to a Black Boy for His Clothes, but Video Shows a White Boy, Dressed Similarly, Was Allowed," CNN, June 24, 2020, https://www.cnn.com/2020/06/23/us/ouzo-bay-baltimore-restaurant-denies-service-to-black-boy-trnd/index.html.

for "being Black while sitting on a park bench."[2] Then there was the man who threatened to call the police on several young Black men working out in the same gym, having assumed that they were not members, though they were.[3] And the list goes on. While incidents like these were nothing new to my son, that they were continuing even amidst protests for racial justice, and the fact that the latest involved a nine-year-old child, seemed to be the last straw for him. "It's all well and good for the NBA and NFL to now pronounce that Black lives matter, but it's too little too late. None of this stuff really makes a difference," he said.

I too wondered what difference the protests and racial reckoning would all really make. As has been shown to this point, the assaults on Black lives are about more than simply policy and politics. They are about a nation's moral imaginary that has become so corrupted by a white way of knowing that affirming Black dignity, let alone Black life, seems hopeless. Perhaps the Afropessimists are right. In fact, in one conversation my son asked what I thought about Afropessimism, as he had just encountered it in his search for answers.

Afropessimism argues that anti-Blackness is so pervasive and deeply ingrained, not simply within systems and structures but in the very psychic framework of the world, that the affirmation of Black humanity is impossible. Frank Wilderson describes Afropessimism as a "meta-theory" that is "pessimistic about the claims theories of liberation make when these theories try to explain Black suffering."[4] This would include Black faith claims

---

2. Matthew Fleisher, "America Is at Its Breaking Point and White Women Still Won't Stop Frivolously Calling Police on Black people," *Los Angeles Times*, June 3, 2020, https://www.latimes.com/opinion/story/2020-06-03/svitlana-flom-amy-cooper-george-floyd-police-racism.

3. "Video of Minnesota Man Threatening to Call Police on Black Entrepreneurs Goes Viral," *The Guardian*, May 27, 2020, https://www.theguardian.com/us-news/2020/may/27/video-minnesota-police-black-entrepreneurs-gym.

4. Frank Wilderson III, *Afropessimism* (New York: Liveright, 2020), Kindle edition, 14.

and the Black theologies of liberation that flow from them. Wilderson says that Black people must face the stark truth that when it comes to Black suffering, "there is no imaginative strategy for redress—no narrative of social, political or national redemption."[5] For Afropessimists there is no hope for a future where Black lives will ever matter. The best option, therefore, is for Black people to accept the reality of Black suffering and to stay alive and sane while trying to navigate it.

Writing decades before the emergence of Afropessimism, philosophical theologian William Jones also recognized the unique nature of Black suffering. For him, Black suffering posed a theodicy question: how to account for the liberatory justice of God in light of the singular magnitude of Black suffering. Jones identified four peculiar characteristics of Black suffering. First, he argued that it was "maldistributed," that is, "it is not spread ...randomly and impartially over the total human race." Second, he said, it had a peculiarly "negative quality" in there was no salvific value to it. Third, he noted its "enormity," given the sheer numbers of people who suffer. Finally, he said that it was "non-catastrophic," that is, not a once-and-for-all event, but "transgenerational, extending over long historical eras."[6]

The profound and unique nature of Black suffering made the theodicy question real for Jones. "Is God a white racist?" he asked, in his book of the same name. "It is my contention," he stated, "that peculiarities of Black suffering make the *question* of divine racism imperative."[7] Adding to this was the fact that Jones could not discern or foresee an "exultation-liberation" event, that is, a time Black people would be freed from their suffering.

---

5. Wilderson, *Afropessimism*, 15.

6. William Jones, *Is God a White Racist? A Preamble to Black Theology* (Garden City, NY: Anchor Press/Doubleday, 1973), 21–22.

7. Jones, *Is God a White Racist?* 22.

"Why has God not eliminated Black suffering?" Jones asked. After determining that God could not be counted on to liberate Black people from the perverse realities of white racism, Jones concluded, "Talk about the inevitable liberation of Blacks must be muted.... Black hope may run afoul of the changing and adapting forms of racism in the future."[8] Jones's words seem prescient given the changing and stubborn realities of white supremacist/anti-Black oppression. From slavery to lynching, to mass incarceration, to police murders, the assaults on Black lives seem only to morph according to the times, but not to end. As Michelle Alexander rightly notes, "Any candid observer of American racial history must acknowledge that racism is highly adaptable." Quoting legal scholar Reva Siegel, Alexander continues, "'Preservation through transformation' is the process through which white privilege is maintained though the rules and rhetoric change."[9]

As my nightly dreams were invaded by images of George Floyd crying out for his mother as he was being suffocated beneath the weight of a white police officer's knee on his neck, and with the gravity of my son's questions unsettling my soul, I found myself making prayerful pleas similar to those Du Bois made decades before:

> Bewildered we are, and passion-tossed, made with the madness of a mobbed and mocked and murdered people; straining at the armposts of Thy Throne, we raise our shackled hands and charge Thee, God, by the bones of our stolen fathers, by the tears of our dead mothers, by the very blood of Thy crucified Christ: *What meaneth this?* Tell us the Plan; give us the Sign!
>
> *Keep not thou silent, O God!*

---

8. Jones, *Is God a White Racist?* 201.

9. Michelle Alexander, *The New Jim Crow: Mass Incarceration in the Age of Colorblindness* (New York/London: The New Press, 2010), 21.

Sit no longer blind, Lord God, deaf to our prayer and dumb to our dumb suffering. Surely Thou, too, art not white, O Lord, a pale, bloodless, heartless thing![10]

At this point, all that was standing between me and the hopeless despair of Afropessimism or a white racist God was my maternal grandmother. Her name was Helen Vivian Dorsey. I've written about her before. My sisters, brother, and I called her Mama. Mama was a poor Black woman who by the age of eighteen was already a widow with a young child, my mother, to rear.

Mama made her way from Atlanta, Georgia, to Columbus, Ohio, during the time when Black people were migrating out of the South in search of a better life. For all the years that I knew Mama, she ran the elevator at the main post office in Columbus. Those were the days in which you literally had to ring a bell for it to come. When it arrived, there was an elevator operator in a starched uniform, sitting on a little stool, who would crank open two gates, ask you which floor you needed to get to, close the gates, and push the proper button to get you to your floor. My grandmother was that operator.

As a child, I thought her job was so "neat," as we used to say. I did not realize how hard it was to be stuck in an elevator eight hours a day, without windows or fresh air, enduring your share of insults, and for a salary that barely kept food on your table. My grandmother hid these hardships from her four grandchildren. No matter how difficult her day might have been, she always made our visits with her fun, even counting out pennies so that we could get treats at the corner store.

I was very close to Mama Dorsey. When she would come to visit, or even when we would visit her, I always found an excuse to sleep with her at night. It was in those nights lying next to her in bed that I got to know about her dream for my siblings and

---

10. W. E. B. Du Bois, "A Litany at Atlanta," in *Darkwaters* (New York: Washington Square Press, 2004), 19.

me. My grandmother's dream was that her four grandchildren would complete high school. This was an audacious dream for a woman who barely had a sixth-grade education and had lived through the time when "white officials believed that only white students needed a high school education and so refused to operate high schools for Black children."[11] Yet, she held fast to her dream, even to the point of setting money aside out of every paycheck for each of her grandchildren to receive after completing high school.

It was in those quiet times before falling off to sleep, as I lay in bed with Mama, that I discovered what fueled her dream and, in fact, kept her going one long day after another. Each night, without fail, I would hear her prayerful whispers thanking God for getting her through another day, and for keeping her grandchildren safe. But most important, I heard her pray that the future would be better for her four grandchildren.

My grandmother did not live long enough to see her dream for her grandchildren come true. She died from a brain aneurysm at the age of fifty-eight, before any of us had finished high school. After her death, however, I was more determined than ever to do my part in making her dream come true—as were my siblings. We each completed high school and much more.

I was equally determined to keep alive within me the faith I had seen in her. But it was getting harder and harder. As assaults on Black life continued, even in the midst of Black Lives Matter protests, I found my faith waning. I wanted to know how in the world my grandmother maintained the hope of faith, the hope in a just God, when everything around her suggested otherwise when it came to Black freedom.

My grandmother witnessed to a faith that was born at the foot of the cross. Black faith is, therefore, a paradox. Even as it

---

11. Nikole Hannah-Jones, "What Is Owed," *New York Times*, June 30, 2020, https://www.nytimes.com/interactive/2020/06/24/magazine/reparations-slavery.html.

was born in the cauldron of slavery, it testifies to the justice of God, and witnesses to the day when "all God's children," even God's Black children, will have shoes. In this sense, Black faith is, in and of itself, a theodicy. It resists any notion that the evil that oppresses Black bodies will have the last word. It proclaims a resounding "No" to the question rightfully raised by Jones, "Is God a white racist?" Knowing this and believing this, however, are two different things. Once again, I was facing a crisis of faith. More than forty years after reading James Cone's proclamation that "Jesus is the Black Christ!" helped me to understand I could be Black with a love for Jesus without contradiction, because in fact Jesus was Black like me, I now wondered if the Black Christ was enough. My son's questions were now my own: "How do we really know that God cares, when Black people are still getting killed?" "How long do we have to wait for the justice of God?" "I get it," my son said, "that Christ is Black, but that doesn't seem to be helping us right now." This chapter is essentially a testimonial response to those questions with the answers I discovered during the summer of Black death and Black protest.

A Resurrecting Invitation

Beyond the image of Jesus on the cross, the other image of him that stands out most to me is of him going off to a lonely place to pray. "But Jesus often withdrew to lonely places and prayed," Luke 5:16 tells us. In fact, of all of the things the disciples witnessed Jesus doing, the only thing they ever asked him to teach them was how to pray.

To pray is to recognize that it is not all up to us, for there is a power that is beyond us. It is through prayer that we can actually reach beyond ourselves to the mystery that is God's transforming power. It is prayer that connects us to God's promise. The fact that we pray perhaps signifies our faith in the God who promises us a more just future. And so, I prayed that God would not keep silent, but would show me the way: "Tell us the plan: give us the sign! *Keep not Thou silent, O God!*"

And then one night after praying, I remembered the words of Jesus: "Do not be afraid. Go and tell my brothers to go to Galilee; there they will see me." In these words, I was being shown the way that I had prayed for. In hearing this invitation of Jesus to his disciples, I realized that I, like them, had been stuck in the crucifying shadow of the cross. The Black Christ that I saw in the faces of George Floyd, Ahmaud Arbery, and Breonna Taylor was a Christ crucified. It was Langston Hughes's "Most Holy Bastard / Of the bleeding mouth / Nigger Christ / On The Cross / of the South."[12] I was literally looking for hope to come "from the blood of Jesus."

As much as I had critiqued models of redemptive suffering, I had unwittingly become trapped in one. Standing before the cross, I found myself relying on the ancient tradition of redemptive sacrificial hope. This is a hope based on the belief that Jesus was sacrificed for human sin. In seeing the crucified Jesus in the faces of murdered Black people, it was as if their Black lives were being sacrificed to redeem the society, if not the world, from the sin of anti-Black white supremacy. As Jesus's crucifixion was a spectacle lynching, so too perhaps was George Floyd's death. Was his life the necessary sacrifice to free the nation and the world from captivity to the original sin of white supremacy? After all, in response to George Floyd's murder, protests had erupted in at least 4,446 cities or towns in the United States and around the globe, all united in demanding that Black lives matter.[13] How many more Black lives would be required to purge the world of this sin?

---

12. Langston Hughes, "Christ in Alabama," in *The Panther and the Lash: Poems of Our Times* (New York: Alfred A. Knopf, 1969), 37.

13. *Mapping Black Lives Matter Protest across the World*, June 20, 2020, https://www.creosotemaps.com/blm2020/.

Religion scholar Biko Mandela Gray is right: "There is something about the way this country lynches and kills Black people for its own salvation that feels Christological in the worst way."[14] This was the Christology I was stuck in, one that allowed for, if not perpetuated, the sacrifice of Black bodies. Black Lives Matter co-founder Patrisse Cullors was right when she said, "We've lived in a place that has literally allowed for us to believe and center only Black death."[15] It was no wonder that my faith was in crisis. I was stuck on the cross that affirmed and centered "Black death."

This is not to minimize the centrality of the cross in Black faith, let alone in my faith. For it is the cross that has made clear to Black people that Jesus is one with them. That Jesus was crucified on the cross is a testament to his utter solidarity with the Black oppressed. It is through the cross that Jesus identifies with the pain and suffering of Black people and that Black Christians have been able to identify with him. Though the cross, as Cone explains, "Jesus makes an unqualified identification with the poor and helpless and takes their pain upon himself."[16] It is for this reason that Black people can sing with authentic passion, "Were you there when they crucified my Lord," with the conviction that that is where they are. Through the cross, the Black experience and Jesus's experience converge. Essentially, the cross shows God's uncompromising solidarity with the Black oppressed even as it reflects the depth of Black oppression. The

---

14. Biko Mandela Gray, "Unwilling Sacrifice: Anti-Blackness, Religion and the Clearing," *Berkley Forum*, June 22, 2020, https://berkleycenter.georgetown.edu/responses/unwilling-sacrifices-anti-blackness-religion-and-the-clearing.

15. Patrisse Cullors and Robert Ross, "The Spiritual Work of Black Lives Matter," *On Being with Krista Tippet*, original air date February 18, 2016, last updated May 25, 2019, https://onbeing.org/programs/patrisse-cullors-and-robert-ross-the-spiritual-work-of-black-lives-matter-may2017/.

16. James Cone, *The Spirituals and the Blues* (Maryknoll, NY: Orbis Books, 1991), 49.

cross does indeed signify to the lynching tree that continues to show itself in new forms, whether as a knee on the neck, being gunned down while jogging, or being murdered during "no-knock" warrant incidents. In Cone's words, "the cross and the lynching tree interpret each other."[17] It was recognizing this connection that to this point had helped me to maintain my faith—for at least I knew that Jesus was one with the Black crucified and not with our white crucifiers. But again, with each new lynching following the last, just knowing this was no longer enough.

Fortunately, the gospel story that Jesus preaches and incarnates does not stop with the cross. Inasmuch as the cross *does* indicate Jesus's utter identification with the oppressed, it is not a static identification. In other words, the fact that Jesus identifies with the oppressed is not a sanctification of oppression, as if it is only in being oppressed that one can find God. Rather, Jesus's identification with the oppressed is an identification with them in their struggle to survive and thrive in the face of the crucifying realities that threaten and destroy their lives. Thus the cross is not the end, but a revelatory point on the way to new life, new reality. It reveals where the movement toward God's just future begins. And if it must begin in crucifying realities, it does not end there. For again, the cross was not the end of Jesus's story, and therefore it did not defeat God's promise for a more just future.

Cone has said, "Though the pain of Jesus' cross was real, there was also joy and beauty in the cross. . . . God's loving solidarity can transform ugliness—whether Jesus on the cross or a lynched Black victim in beauty, into God's liberating presence." Through the powerful imagination of faith, we can discover, the "terrible beauty" of the cross and the "tragic beauty" of the lynching tree. There is something beyond the cross that shows

---

17. James Cone, *The Cross and the Lynching Tree* (Maryknoll, NY: Orbis Books, 2011), 161.

us the joy and beauty of "God's liberating presence." That which lies beyond the cross is in fact what Black church people testify to in song when they sing, "Weeping may endure for a night, but joy cometh in the morning." The cross alone simply does not allow us to imagine a new life that is not predicated on Black sacrificial death. The cross is about death. The "joy and beauty of God's liberation presence" are about life. Again, the words of Patrisse Cullors are instructive:

> We've forgotten how to imagine black life. Literally, whole human beings have been rendered to die prematurely, rendered to be sick, and we've allowed for that. Our imagination has only allowed for us to understand black people as a dying people. We have to change that. That's our collective imagination. Someone imagined handcuffs; someone imagined guns; someone imagined a jail cell. Well, how do we imagine something different that actually centers black people, that sees them in the future? Let's imagine something different.[18]

In asking his disciples to meet him in Galilee, Jesus was indeed calling them to imagine something different for the world. Jesus was asking them to imagine a world where life, not death, is centered.

Essentially, Jesus's calling of the disciples back to Galilee was an affirmation not simply that the cross does not have the last word, but that it is not where salvation and redemption for the world are to be found. The site of salvation is not Golgotha's hill. Salvation is to be found in what womanist theologian Delores Williams calls Jesus's "ministerial vision." Williams explains: "Jesus did not come to redeem humans by showing them God's 'love' manifested in the death of God's innocent child on a cross erected by cruel, imperialistic, patriarchal power. Rather, . . . the spirit of God in Jesus came to show humans *life*—to show

---

redemption through a perfect *ministerial* vision." The cross, Williams adds, was "the evil of humankind trying to kill the *ministerial vision....* The cross only represents historical evil trying to defeat good."[19] This ministerial vision is a vision of the new life of God's promised future. It is in this vision that salvation is found. To reiterate, that Jesus was resurrected shows that even the evil of the cross could not stop the vision. Therefore, it cannot be said enough that the cross does not sanctify the sacrifice of Black life. Quite the contrary. The very fact that Black lives are victims of crucifying death is an affront to God's very vision.

On the one hand, there is no clearer indication of the breach between the world as it is and the world as God has called it to be than the fact that Black life continues to be "worth a half-cent." Yet, on the other hand, there is no clearer indication of the hope that Black life will one day matter than in the resurrection. Williams puts it this way: "The resurrection of Jesus and the flourishing of God's spirit in the world as the result of the resurrection represent the life of the *ministerial vision* gaining victory over the evil attempt to kill it."[20] Simply put, the way to a new moral imaginary that "actually centers Black life" is not the way of Jesus's death on the cross, but the way of his resurrected life. This is why the enslaved sang:

> De angel roll de stone away
> De angel roll de stone away
> 'Twas on a bright an' shiny morn
> When de trumpet begin to soun'
> De angel roll de stone away
>
> Sister Mary came a-running at de break o' day
> Brought de news f'om heab'n

---

19. Dolores S. Williams, *Sisters in the Wilderness: The Challenges of Womanist God-Talk* (Maryknoll, NY: Orbis Books, 1993), 164–65.

20. Williams, *Sisters in the Wilderness*, 165.

De stone done roll away
I'm a-lookin' for my Savior, tell me where He lay
High up on de mountain
De stone done roll away.[21]

And this is why Jesus called his disciples to Galilee. The Resurrected Jesus resurrected his disciples by inviting them away from the despair of death that was the cross into the hope of new life that was the resurrection. A community that had given up on the possibilities for life, that had lost faith in the gospel that Jesus preached, was called back into life-giving ministry. This is what the invitation to Galilee was all about.

When I remembered this Galilean invitation, as I stood in my own existential despair of crucifying Black deaths, it was as if I was being invited to Galilee to meet the resurrected Jesus. Not knowing where else to go, I put on my mask and I went down to Black Lives Matter Plaza on 16th and K in Washington, DC, right down from the White House. And it was there—in the midst of a mosaic of people witnessing with shouts, signs, and singing that Black Lives Matter—that something happened. I literally found myself laughing.

A Laughing God

Peter Berger has described laughing as a "signal of transcendence." Signals of transcendence, Berger explains, are "phenomena that are to be found within the domain of our 'natural' reality but that appear to point beyond that reality." They are "gestures" that signal a world that transcends "the normal, everyday world."[22] In this instance, they are those signals from

---

21. See https://www.negrospirituals.com/songs/de_angel_roll_de_stone_away.htm.

22. Peter Berger, *A Rumor of Angels: Modern Society and the Rediscovery of the Supernatural* (Garden City, NY: Doubleday, 1969), 53.

God indicating that there is a just future beyond the unjust present. Berger identifies laughter as one of those signals because, as the product of humor, it points to an almost absurd discrepancy. "Discrepancy," Berger says, "is the stuff of which jokes are made."[23] Furthermore, Berger adds, laughter "mocks the 'serious' business of this world and the mighty who carry it on.... It relativizes the seemingly rocklike necessities of this world."[24]

As I stood surrounded by the people on Black Lives Matter Plaza proclaiming that Black lives mattered, steps away from the very White House that was espousing a vision to "Make America Great Again," a vision that promised Black death—all I could do was laugh. My laughter was a signal of transcendence recognizing the discrepancy of the present that was the MAGA vision and the future that was God's vision where Black lives would matter. That I found myself reflexively laughing was like a signal from God "mocking" and relativizing the MAGA vision. My laughter was a reminder that the MAGA vision would not have the last word. The clearest indication of this truth was this Black Lives Matter demonstration taking place steps from the White House on a street with the words "Black Lives Matter" boldly emblazoned on it.

Humanist Anthony Pinn has rightly recognized that there is a gap "between white lies and Black life mattering." He goes on to say that Christianity "offers nothing unique to service the demands of this particular moment that seeks racial justice."[25] In other words, he says that Christianity has nothing to "mind that gap." In that moment of laughter, I discovered anew what Christianity actually does have to mind the gap between a present of Black death and a future where Black life mattered: it is

---

23. Berger, *Rumor of Angels*, 69–70.

24. Berger, *Rumor of Angels*, 70–71.

25. "Mind the Gap: Humanist Thoughts on Christianity in the Age of Black Lives Matter," *Berkley Forum*, June 22, 2020, https://berkleycenter. georgetown. edu/responses/mind-the-gap-humanist-thoughts-on-christianity-in-the-age-of-black-lives-matter.

resurrecting hope. As I stood there in what seemed like a sea of people, my laughter was nothing less than a signal of transcendence pointing me to the resurrecting hope that had disrupted the seeming futility of crucifying Black death. And, as I looked around—there it was right in front of me.

The first thing that struck me was that I was witnessing a global movement. This protest in Washington, DC, was one of thousands across the globe. For instance, people in Sydney, Australia, took up the cry for Black lives to matter as they demanded an end to the death of Black people in the custody of Australian police. One mother said, "I am going to keep marching until we get justice for my son." Her son was twenty-six when he "died after five guards rushed into his cell to stop him eating biscuits, dragged him to another cell, held him face down and injected him with a sedative."[26] Hundreds of protesters also took to the streets in London. As one of these protesters said, "Once we see there's actual true intention to protect the lives of Black people and change systemic suffering, we will stop marching and we will work with the government."[27]

People in numerous countries across Africa also joined the protest. There were even protests in those African countries where, according to Mokey Makura, director of the Pan Africa Collaborative "Africa No Filter," they "don't have that same clear dichotomy of Black and white racism." Nevertheless, she said, "what we do have on the continent is colonialism and in both cases, with racism and with colonialism, it's the white perpetrator and the Black victim. . . . So I feel there's a lot of empathy with the situation our American brothers are experiencing

---

26. "Sydney's Black Lives Matter Protest to Go Ahead Despite Organisers Losing Court Appeal," *The Guardian*, July 27, 2020, https://www.theguardian.com/australia-news/2020/jul/27/sydneys-black-lives-matter-protest-to-go-ahead-despite-organisers-losing-court-appeal.

27. "Hundreds Join March to Protest against Systemic Racism in the UK," *The Guardian*, August 30, 2020, https://www.theguardian.com/world/2020/aug/30/hundreds-join-march-to-protest-against-systemic-racism-in-the-uk.

now."[28] There were also protests across Asia. As one reporter explained, in Asia "protesters are not only taking to the streets in solidarity with those in America, but also *highlighting ongoing inequalities and discrimination within the region.* Some are also highlighting the hypocrisy of leaders who are vocal about #BlackLivesMatter in the United States but carry on perpetuating ongoing inequality in their own countries."[29]

Religious studies professor Joseph Winters has called these global protests in response to George Floyd's murder "expressions of kinetic energy, energy that can be directed toward goals but that also exceeds what can be actualized and rendered concrete."[30] I agree with Winters that these protests do reflect movements erupting around the globe in response to other movements. Yet, I do not agree that they reflect demands that cannot be "actualized and rendered concrete." Rather, these protests reflect confidence that there can be a world where Black lives will matter—despite the crucifying realities of the present. In this regard, the protests are more aptly defined as expressions of *resurrecting contagion.*

René Girard uses the word "contagion" as a part of his wider theory on mimetics and sacrifice. On one hand, contagion points to the negative forces that spread within a community, resulting in violence. On the other hand, violence itself serves as a contagion, as it then spreads within a community. Girard explains, "There is something about the spectacle of violence. Indeed, at times it is impossible to stay immune from its

---

28. Peter Dowd and Allison Hagan, "Black Lives Matter Movement Resonates across Africa," *Here and Now,* June 12, 2020, https://www.wbur.org/hereandnow/2020/06/12/black-lives-matter-africa.

29. Nithin Coca, "Supporting Black Lives Matter in Asia," *Asia Undercovered,* August 17, 2020, https://medium.com/asiaundercovered/supporting-black-lives-matter-in-asia-912ef72ce3f1.

30. Joseph Winters, "Black Lives Matter: Between Novelty and Repetition," *Berkley Forum,* June 22, 2020, https://berkleycenter.georgetown.edu/responses/black-lives-matter-between-novelty-and-repetition.

infection."[31] Girard further argues that as violence spreads, it also builds. In other words, violence leads to violence, and each new instance of violence is more intense than the one before. Girard concludes: "Violence [is] something eminently communicable. ...The slightest outbreak of violence," he says, "can bring about a catastrophic escalation."[32] It is within the framework of "mimetic sacrificial contagion" that Girard understands the growing violence that culminated in Jesus's crucifixion.

While for Girard contagion has negative connotations, it can connote the spread of something positive as well, like the spread of laughter. It is often the case that seeing a person laugh will make another person laugh—and on it goes. It is in this way that I view the Black Lives Matter protests as "resurrecting contagion." Not only did they make me laugh but they were infectiously spreading around the globe, as if they were the laughter of God. As these protests spread like a contagion, they demanded conditions within each particular locality that would foster Black life. It was as if the resurrecting God was resurrecting communities around the globe from the despair of crucifying death into the resurrecting hope of new life.

Essentially, the protests signaled a contagion of an imaginary that envisioned what theologian Ashton Crawley calls an "otherwise possibility" for Black life in a world that can imagine only Black death. "Otherwise possibility," as Crawley explains, "is not utopic...but it is the elaboration of the fact that an alternative exists."[33] It reflects a "mode of constituting otherwise ways of being in the world."[34] And this leads me to the second aspect of the protests that I noticed in my laughter.

---

31. René Girard, *Violence and the Sacred*, translated by Patrick Gregory (Baltimore: Johns Hopkins University Press, 1977), 30.

32. Girard, *Violence and the Sacred*, 30.

33. Ashton T. Crawley, *The Lonely Letters* (Durham, NC, and London: Duke University Press, 2020), 29.

34. Crawley, *Lonely Letters*, 30.

Standing in that small space of Black Lives Matter Plaza in front of the White House was the most motley and diverse crew of God's sacred creation that I had seen come together in protest. They reflected an "otherwise way of being in the world." They were Black, white, brown, Asian and non-Asian, Latinx and non-Latinx, queer and non-queer, trans and non-trans, bi-gendered and non-bi-gendered. They were also young and old and everything in between. As I walked through the crowd, there was a clear common cause. There was no claiming of privilege or rank. People were there advocating, each in their own way, for a world that looked more like God's just future: a future where all people were living in the peace that was justice. They were embodying that very future.

Pauli Murray, the first Black woman priest in the Episcopal Church, says, "True community is based upon equality, mutuality and reciprocity. It affirms the richness of individual diversity as well as the common human ties that bind us together."[35] True community is nothing less than the future that God calls us to. It was this true community that was on display at Black Lives Matter Plaza. And so, when I heard the chant go up, "This is what Democracy looks like!" I laughed even harder, before joining in the chant. Insofar as the protesters that day were a glimpse of God's just future, they reflected what democracy could look like within the vision of this nation's better angels. Bayard Rustin once said, "If we desire a society that is democratic, then democracy must become a means as well as an end."[36] The protest that day on the Plaza was a democratic means in protest for a democratic society.

---

35. "Why You Don't Know Who Pauli Murray Is and Why You Should," *Represent Women*, July 3, 2017, https://www.representwomen.org/why_you_don_t_know_who_pauli_murray_is_and_why_you_should.

36. Bayard Rustin, "Letter to the Children of Cleveland, Dec. 3, 1969," quoted in Michael Long, "Bayard Rustin in His Own Words: 'I Must Resist,'" *Huffington Post*, March 15, 2013, updated February 2, 2016, https://www.huffpost.com/entry/bayard-rustin-in-his-own_b_ 2881057.

As I was walking away from Black Lives Matter Plaza to head home, I realized that the protest, along with other Black Lives Matter protests around the globe, was itself a signal of transcendence. Various people have commented on the religious and spiritual aspects of the Black Lives Matter movement. In doing so, they have pointed to the rituals and practices that usually accompany the protests, as well as the way in which they are described by many of the Black Lives Matter organizers. Hebah Farrag, a researcher of various spiritual movements, describes the various rituals of kneeling in prayer, calling out the names of Black lives lost, as well as the pouring of libations as examples of practices carried out at many of the protests that point to their spiritual meaning. After observing many of these practices, she concludes:

> The movement for Black lives sees itself as the current embodiment in a legacy of spirit-infused social justice work. There is a veneration for the sacred duty of the freedom fighter and a dream for the day it will no longer be necessary.... The movement for Black lives works towards the goal of not just racial justice, but freedom of the mind and the spirit. It encourages "healing justice," so that people can heal from trauma and engage as the best version of themselves. The movement infuses a syncretic blend of African and indigenous cultures' spiritual practices and beliefs, embracing ancestor worship; Ifa-based ritual such as chanting, dancing, and summoning deities; and healing practices such as acupuncture, reiki, therapeutic massage, and plant medicine in much of its work, including protest.[37]

Patrisse Cullors also describes the Black Lives Matter movement as a "spiritual movement," noting that many of the actions

---

37. Hebah Farrag, "The Fight for Black Lives Is a Spiritual Movement," June 9, 2020, *Berkley Forum*, https://berkleycenter.georgetown.edu/responses/the-fight-for-black-lives-is-a-spiritual-movement.

are "deeply spiritual." She describes them as "often led by opening prayer. Folks are usually sage-ing. We use a lot of indigenous practices. People build altars to people who have passed.
And so it's this moment to both stand face-to-face with law enforcement, but it's also this moment to be deeply reflective on
the people who've been killed by the state and give them our
honor. It's an honor to protest for them."[38] More particularly, she
calls the movement a form of "healing justice." She explains that
not only is the movement attempting to transform society to be
a place that fosters Black life and life-giving relationships, but
also it is transforming the participants in the movement. It's
healing for them, she says, because they can "show up" in the
work as their "whole selves."[39]

There is no doubt that the Black Lives Matter protests are
rich with spiritual rituals, practices, and profound meanings,
but it was not those things that led me to recognize the movement of protest as a signal of transcendence. Rather, it was because it reflects a movement of hope. And hope, Berger states, is
indeed a signal of transcendence. It points to the possibilities to
"overcome the difficulties of any given here and now." Berger
goes on to say that "the profound manifestations of hope are to
be found in gestures of courage undertaken in defiance of
death." There was, for me, no greater witness to hope than those
protesters gathering in the face of anti-Black/white supremacist
Black death (not to speak of the raging pandemic), coming out
to protest for the just life that God promises us all.

To laugh is a signal of transcendence. It is that which signals
a discrepancy between what is and what ought to be, the discrepancy between our unjust present and God's just future. And
so it is that God's resurrection of Jesus after his crucifying death
was nothing other than God's last laugh over the crucifying

---

38. Cullors and Ross, "Spiritual Work of Black Lives Matter."
39. Cullors and Ross, "Spiritual Work of Black Lives Matter."

powers of evil that declare their "greatness" in our world. As I walked away from Black Lives Matter Plaza, through the music, the singing, and the chants, I heard God's laughter of resurrection: "Ha-ha, ha, you lose, you will not have the last word—Black lives will matter in this world."

I had gone down to Black Lives Matter Plaza that day filled with the despair of crucifying Black death. But, as it turned out, the Black Lives Matter Plaza was my Galilee. It was there that I did indeed find the movement that was the resurrected Jesus. Vincent Lloyd is right when he says, "The deepest meaning of Black Lives Matter is a call for new life rather than better life, for conversion rather than improvement. It is a call for life to be lived in a way that does not give death the final word."[40] I walked away from Black Lives Matter Plaza laughing. I walked away filled with the Resurrection Hope of Black life.

A Hopeful End

If Black life is ever to matter in this country one thing is clear: it demands a moral imaginary that can contain the vision of God's just future. Anything short of that signals a nation, a people, still held captive to anti-Black white supremacist sin. I have no illusions, as this book has shown, that the task will be easy. It will require a steadfast commitment to doing the work that will carry on well beyond the protest to overcome a "white way of knowing" that stands in the way of any notion of Black equality. Inasmuch as the Protestant work ethic has any salience, it is in recognizing that work is indicative of God's salvation. In this instance, it is the work that joins with God in redeeming the world

---

40. "What a Time to Be Alive: The Work of Mourning and the Privilege of Black Death," ABC *Religion and Ethics*, June 15, 2020, https://www.abc.net.au/religion/vincent-lloyd-the-privilege-of-black-deaths/12357138.

from the original sin that "raced" God's people into those who deserve life and those who do not.

While shrouded in the sin of anti-Black/white supremacy, this nation did give birth to a vision in which all people could enjoy their God-given rights to "life, liberty, and the pursuit of happiness." This is a vision that takes us just a little bit closer to the just future that God promises us all. When I was on Black Lives Matter Plaza, I realized that this vision had not died on the crosses on which too many Black lives had been crucified. Paraphrasing the words of abolitionist preacher Theodore Parker, Martin Luther King Jr. said that "the arc of the moral universe is long, but it bends toward justice." While I was down on Black Lives Matter Plaza, I felt that, yes, the protests were a sign of a people getting on that arc, but more than that, they were a sign of God's justice bending down toward the earth to open up the moral imaginary of what was possible. What was possible was the crowd so gathered.

As I was riding home from my time at the Plaza, I called my son. When he answered the phone I simply said, "Desmond, yes these protests do make a difference, because they are God's laugh, letting us know that there will be a future where Black lives will matter."

AFTERWORD

The Final Conversation

As the summer went on and protests ended, but Black deaths did not end, my son asked, "How, really, do you keep hoping? You lived through the 1960s, and here we are again. Are you just tired of it all?"

I answered by telling him about his great-great-grandmother. We called her Mama Mary. Mama Mary was born into slavery. She died when I was around six years old. Every time I think about Mama Mary, I think of those Black people who were born into slavery, died in slavery, and never drew a free breath. In fact, they never dreamt that they would ever breathe a free breath. Yet, they fought for freedom anyhow. They fought for a freedom that they knew they would never see, but still believed that it would in fact one day be. They fought for a freedom that was nothing less than the freedom that is the justice of God. This was their hope—a hope that was found and lived out in their struggle for freedom—for it was in that struggle that they met God, even in the midst of slavery. Theirs is a resurrecting hope, because when I think of them and their fight for freedom, I cannot give in to that which would destroy Black life. It is because of their hope that I am here writing this book.

This is what I told my son.

INDEX